My Second Twenty Years

My Second Twenty Years

An Unexpected Life

RICHARD P. BRICKNER

Basic Books, Inc., Publishers   New York

Library of Congress Cataloging in Publication Data

Brickner, Richard P.
  My second twenty years.

  1. Brickner, Richard P   Autobiography. I. Title.
PS3552.R45Z52   813′.5′4   [B]   76–10972
ISBN: 0–465–04773–4

Acknowledgments

A grant for 1974–75 from the National Foundation for the Arts helped significantly to support the writing of this book and is deeply appreciated. Likewise, the distinguished advice and encouragement of Nancy Harrow Krukowski, Betty Anne Clarke, Theodore Solotaroff, and Erwin Glikes. My mother, Ruth Brickner, M.D., was of crucial help in supplying and confirming certain material. Her loving interest and her objectivity were, as they have long been, of the greatest benefit to me.

A small part of this book appeared, in different form, in *American Review* 19, January 1974.

My Second Twenty Years

ONE

IN MAY OF 1953, a few days after my twentieth birthday, I broke my neck in an automobile accident and lay for a while, precariously, on the farthest rim of existence.

Even if one happens to be the offspring of two psychiatrists, as I am, one is not necessarily convinced that accidents must be self-willed. The son of two psychiatrists, in fact, may resist the idea all the more; so may the psychiatrists. True, I was driving the car; I drove it off the road, causing it to flip over. Still, when I return from time to time to the scene of my youth, I whisper into the wings to Freud, "You are wrong, there are accidents, pure and accidental." My accident happened with a suddenness beyond my control, out of the blue.

In retrospect, though, signs that I wanted an interruption to my panicky youth mark the examined blue. We all know about retrospect, how it shames the blindness of one approaching a transforming event. Accidents happen "before we knew it." After twenty-odd years of retrospection, of attempting to "know it," I am still investigating causes. I still find new questions to ask. The more time that passes, the fuller my mental archives become.

Did I "have" the accident or did it have me? Did I want to go back to the beginning or beyond? Was I scared to grow up? If I was scared to grow up, then why was my behavior at eighteen, nineteen, so furiously imitative of "grown-up" behavior? Why, at college, was I acting like a literary master (acting even more like a critic than a writer—how better to seem a literary master when my mature production consisted of a half-dozen poems and half a story)? And why was I acting so married to my girlfriend, the first girl not a whore I had ever gone to bed with? Margaret, who helped fulfill my yearning for maturity by being a year ahead of me, had platinum hair and, as my mother encouragingly pointed out, "beautiful skin." But it was her exotic and ample body of literary and musical knowledge that went straight to my groin. Sex with Margaret was gravy; a spoonful. Her diffident sexuality, a torment to me, was at the same time nearly a virtue, according to my sense that we were supposed to be, as adults, beyond ardor. Why was I trying to hurry away from my youth? It occurs to me that my father's three heart attacks, the third of which took place six weeks before the accident, must have been giving me the main push over thin ice to the adult side. I felt imperiled and rushed, as if I were failing a sub-conscious crash course—its invisible teacher as ignorant as I of the subject—in how to replace my father. I felt also as if the nightmare-thin ice under my klutzy feet had been laid down by a bully: however much I may have wished my father to die, I didn't want to be tortured by the possibility. Die, don't die, but *decide.*

The day before the accident, Margaret and I had a bad fight that ended in gloom. We fought a great deal, usually on account of her discomfort at having sex with me in the off-campus apartment I had taken for my sophomore year at Middlebury College with my friend Mike. The apartment made sex possible, but never certain. Margaret was rebellious because people "knew," and because I was in an incessant state of tyrannical heat. (Repeated scene: Margaret stomping out of the apartment, scurrying up the hill toward her dorm; I following slowly a block back—not deserving, not wanting, to catch up with her—calling, "Margaret, please! Stop a minute! For God's sake, *listen* to me!") If we were beyond ardor, and we were, from the beginning, I had not yet managed to get lust behind me. At the end of the fight that day, she asked me to hit her. My hand fell against her cheek in a clumsy pat. We should have known by then that our relationship wasn't worth its exhausting unhappiness, and probably we did but were too eager to prove that we could correct our errors. Later in the afternoon, Mike roared me around the outskirts of Middlebury in his red MG. I took the wheel for a stretch, trying to learn to drive the thing, trying to do my own roaring.

Mike was casually classy: the MG, a camel's hair coat that sometimes looked—this impressed me a good deal—as if he were using it for dusting; an adorable, doe-faced girlfriend, so unlike self-conscious Margaret, cheerful, her sexuality pleased with itself. Mike was too easy-going, but gave me the impression that he kicked at his laziness. He could be irritable, and, in the hiking boots he invariably wore, he pounded rather than walked, seeming to confirm a potentiality for anger. He clearly enjoyed life, however, more than he was irritated at himself, and I enjoyed watching him do that. I think he respected my earnest involvement with experience, my hardworking hope to make meaning of it in the labored, congested poems I wrote (and published in "Frontiers," Middlebury's literary magazine), and in my literature and music courses. I think he respected me for taking everything hard, much as he must have seen, and been amused, that I overdid it. Mike could have become the kind of man whose villa artists like to frequent. Not that I, young artist, lived off him. We inhabited a bohemian basement slum, with catshit in the couch and prints taped to the ceiling. But I breathed his air of relative ease. I relaxed with him. He must have suggested to me—in his social flexibility, his pleasure in pleasure, and his informal intellectuality—my high school friends, my old New York City self.

The MG was a kiddie car; one sat low in it, as if on the road. But when Mike would drive me to class, I felt elevated and enlarged, protected, a triumphant puzzlement to the campus bour-

geoisie I despised and feared. I imagined I appeared less prig-
gishly aloof when I was a passenger in the MG.

The day after our fight, Margaret and I made up and decided
to go that evening to the movies, *Moulin Rouge*, José Ferrer as
Toulouse Lautrec. And later, Mike and I went out for another
driving lesson, and the accident occurred.

My father once told me he blamed himself for what happened, because he hadn't taught me how to drive. I don't recall
what I replied, something reassuring, most likely. I doubt that I
told him my mother had taught me to drive, more or less, in her
Ford. I doubt that he ever knew of these lessons. They were the
sort of thing one instinctively kept from him. If my father had
ever offered to teach me, I would have wanted, but been unable,
to say no. My father was the sort of man who finds it intolerable to be driven by anyone else at all, so it is impossible for
me to see him sitting instructively by the side of a terrified son
who lacked any mechanical instinct, who was virtually oblivious
to physical cause and effect. As a child, I once jumped from a
high rock, holding an umbrella over my head. I didn't imagine
that my wind would be knocked out, or that I could have broken
my legs. I got myself clubbed to the ground more than I should
have by running into trees and walls. And I often slammed car
doors, having arrived somewhere, without looking behind me,
my carelessness provoking my father to rage. My carelessness, his
rage; his rage, my repeated carelessness. He taught me that if I
was indifferent to other people's fingers, inattentive to his rage,
I'd get to him. Nothing, certainly not love, prevents parents and
children from harming one another.

On a long, straight road beyond Middlebury, I again took over
the wheel of the MG. It was a gorgeous Vermont May afternoon,
green and yellow, light and still. I turned left down a hill, feeling knowledgeable. I pressed on the brake, as I thought, but as
I kept pressing we picked up speed. The brake and the clutch
of the MG, like the wheel, are in reverse of their American positions, and I was pumping the clutch. Either because I thought it

was the only way to stop the car or because I had suspended thinking, I tumbled us into a ditch. By then we must have been going faster than I remember we were going; Mike didn't have time to set us straight. In the ditch the car tipped over, and I was thrown out of it, onto the road.

The instant my head hit the road, I felt my muscles drain away. The sensation lasted as long as an X-ray takes. Without trying to move, I knew I couldn't move. Or trying to move was being unable to move. Trying, not trying, amounted to the same thing. I saw Mike standing over me. I shouted at him, "I can't move! Am I going to die?" I shouted because my question was reasonable. Mike sounded convinced when he said I wasn't going to die, even though I couldn't move and even though he could see the blood in my hair. In fact, the head wound was not, by itself, serious, but, from the scar, I know it made a semi-circle, ear to ear.

Boys came running from a field. We told them to get help fast. I have sometimes imagined them as they were running off, imagined that there must have been giddy terror in their legs, a hysterical sense that speed wasn't sufficient. Running to a house, a telephone, if I had been one of them, I would have been think-ing that all the running I'd ever done while pretending to be scared was preparation for this unforeseeable moment, when a strange man lay on his back with a bloody head in the once peaceful, once familiar road.

Hovering at length over the scene as I write about it, I think repeatedly of Auden's poem "Musée des Beaux Arts," in which Breughel's *Icarus* is described:

> . . . how everything turns away
> Quite leisurely from the disaster; the ploughman may
> Have heard the splash, the forsaken cry,
> But for him it was not an important failure; the sun shone
> As it had to on the white legs disappearing into the green

Water; and the expensive delicate ship that must have seen
Something amazing, a boy falling out of the sky,
Had somewhere to get to and sailed calmly on.

The lines freeze me with the knowledge of how it could have
been, how it could have been when my head hit the road, and
how it could have been later. My luck was as good as it was bad.
I had always lived with a net under me. From the moment those
boys went running off in alarm to telephone for an ambulance,
I had the sense that I was being saved; and the sense of salvation is part of salvation. I wasn't left alone in the middle of the
road, in a semblance of death, only silence, trees, around me.
Mike could stay by me. Even when, a few days later, I actually
began to die, one of the reasons I did not die is that I felt I was
meant to be saved. I was surrounded by incessant motions of
support. It was like being celebrated. I might have been a stranger to earth, who had hurtled from space at a misjudged speed,
and was being helped to survive by humans.

I remember, next, lying on an examining table in the Porter
Hospital in Middlebury, waiting for the neurosurgeon to come
from Burlington and sew up my scalp. It was then late afternoon. Arthur Healey, the head of the Middlebury Art Department, looked in the door. The campus had heard. Healey ob-
served that the color of my blood matched the color of the sunset.
When Dr. Donaghy arrived from Burlington, I warned him to
bear in mind, calling my parents, that my father had had a heart
attack only six weeks before; Donaghy should speak to my
mother and let her tell my father. I could kill my father now, I
felt.

My mother has told me that, on hearing from Donaghy, she
"melted like wax" to the floor. Another touch of Icarus. My
younger sister was in the room with her, helped her up. My
father was out on his first drive since recovering from his attack.
When my mother heard his car returning, she went down to the
kitchen to tell him. He listened calmly, and went to the phone

and called Donaghy. Then he called another neurosurgeon, his friend and colleague, Lee Davidoff.

My mother and Leo Davidoff flew to Burlington the next morning. My father, on medical advice, drove up. I traveled there on my back in an ambulance. The Middlebury doctor, Walker, sat beside me. He fed me a cigarette. I would be fed everything for months, be on my back for months.

I liked Dr. Walker because he was with me, because he hadn't refused me the cigarette, because the year before he'd come to see me in my dormitory room when I'd been rejected by Bea, the girl preceding Margaret. I was a statue of depression at the time. But when he asked me if I felt suicidal, I answered no, without deliberation. The spontaneity of my answer assured me that despite my inclination to alarm myself, and dramatize my alarm, I would much rather suffer along with the rest of humanity—little as I understood what that meant—than push my self-importance. I liked Dr. Walker for the seriousness of the question he had asked me, and for the modesty of my response. It didn't occur to me, in the ambulance, to ask myself whether I had changed my mind since, or whether my original answer had been honest.

At about noon, I was slid into the Mary Fletcher Hospital in Burlington and delivered to a bed I could not get out of and could do nothing in. Donaghy and Davidoff consulted. Donaghy had already decided that surgery to relieve pressure of spinal column on spinal cord would be useless and was opting for the use of traction. Davidoff agreed. When they examined me, they found that I had one touch of sensation, at the penis, indicating that my spinal cord was not severed, which meant the chance for some recovery. (Beyond ardor *and* heat, but not hope.) I waited for my father, and for the crisis that was collecting in my body.

My father's second heart attack had struck him while he was on a fishing vacation with my mother, just before my departure for Middlebury as a freshman. He was taken to a hospital in Watertown, New York. From home I wrote to my mother at the hospital: "To come up before college would be possible but very difficult. Without going into details too much, the distance that would have to be covered all in all is considerable, and though I don't know the bus connections, on the map it doesn't look too good. . . . Once I am settled, I'm sure I'll be able to come—it's only an eight-hour bus trip and costs ten bucks. [How did I know this if I didn't know the bus connections?] I will write frequently and keep you informed on what's happening. I think Dad will understand that even though I would like to see him very much it would be a terrific inconvenience at the present moment." The next day I wrote: "There are bus connections, Middlebury to Watertown, which means an all-night bus trip." I asked my mother to write to the Dean of Men at Middlebury, getting his permission for me to take two days out of the orientation period. "This will be before classes start, enable me to get settled, and eliminate the terrific rush and exhaustion that a trip right away would mean. You will understand that this decision has come after a lot of thought and I hope it seems sensible to both Dad and you. It is positively the best I can do. . . . Tell Dad I am sorry, that we have tried every way and that this is the only one at all feasible. My deepest, sonniest love to both of you." I never went.

The accident left me on the farthest rim of existence but did not, finally, push me off; I dropped, then, from that rim onto a plain of physical infancy. The accident gave me both the impetus and a chance to start a second time, to "do it over," as if I had been granted a mythic wish. What is different about me is that I was reincarnated. I have a double history and a view of this double history that makes it, for me, a destiny. I remember my first life, my other twenty years, well, and often review family scenes in which I prepared for my adulthood-to-have-been.

My father, at least apparently, had the larger role of the two parents. In fact, a larger role than my own. I loved my father, admired him, was frightened of him most of the time. He never hit me, but his impatience sizzled, often striking me in painful splats. In the morning, he yelled and slammed doors if he was awakened by my brother or sister or me running (or for his sake creeping) downstairs, or if the talcum powder was missing from his bathroom. In the evenings, there would be an earthquake if a bicycle were in the driveway, or if dinner were late. The foundations of our home seemed to me vulnerable. Very early, I became self-conscious around my father. I was once trotting down a steep, narrow stairway and saw him heading up. I realized, terrified, that I was chewing gum. My father hated the chewing of gum as one hates being spit at. I swallowed the gum, passing him close. He would not have punished me if he'd caught me chewing. He was not a punisher. But my sense of his lurking rage was enough to keep me preposterously nervous. I felt, in the house with him, as if I had miraculously remembered to wipe my muddy feet on the doormat but was leaving tracks on the rug anyway. No matter how carefully I watched my step, I made mistakes—dropped things, bumped things, forgot things. The man who kissed me, who called me, to my pleasure, "Dickie-bird," who loved me for my evident sunniness, who, in his work, "made people better," was often, to me, a Hitler, a physically bigger Hitler, a worse Hitler. His occasional rages at my mother over a missing this or an insufficient that brought me to tears of anger, but I could not say a word to him. Later, I would yell at my mother (already once yelled at), "How can you let him do that to you?" In 1945, when the real Hitler disappeared, my aggrieved twelve-year-old mind tried hard for a while to figure out a sensible proof for my conviction that the world's most evil man was now hiding out in my father's skin. At thirteen, I came home from school one day and informed my mother that our class had been told we were entering the rebellious stage. "No hard feelings," I said, and shook her hand. This apology in advance was the end of my adolescent rebellion. But I had the satisfaction—it was like "biting down" at the dentist's—of knowing that I hated my father and that I was justified in hating him. Once, I saw him on a street in the city and turned a corner so that he wouldn't see me. An invisible snub.

Out of his sight, I acted up. I was most free of him when I performed. Not only in high school plays or, for two seasons, in summer stock, or with my friends on the street, where we did a lot of elaborate improvising, but during football games (one eye on the stands) and in classrooms, where my many questions, though usually serious, were often a quite conscious way for me to get the floor, as much as to get or give information. I would love to ask questions on subjects I thought the teacher was avoiding.

My father caught me in my act when he attended a performance of the high school chorus, in which I sang tenor. Afterward, with frustrated, querulous gestures, he lit into me for bobbing my head ostentatiously to the music, charged me with making a fool of myself. No doubt I'd had my eye on the audience; no doubt I was also involved with the beat. My father did not understand how desperate I was for definition; or else my desperation upset him. He mashed the evening.

The fear of my father's heart trouble, the grudge I had clutched through the years against his domestic tyranny, which made it possible for me to write those grandiosely selfish letters to the hospital in Watertown and not to make the trip there, were now going to be softened and shamed. My father was going to do wholly for me what I had shirked altogether doing for him. Whatever anger or self-pity he may have felt after the catastrophic climax of the very blitheness and ineptitude in me that had always enraged him, he gave me only his best self: he was tender, undespairing; and, a neurologist as well as psychiatrist, he was also able to be specifically energetic and imaginative. It may be that he realized, on his drive up to Burlington, that he had helped me reach the point where he could lose me: not by failing to teach me how to drive but by teaching me, through the firmness of his tyranny, to be careless, inattentive, elsewhere, an "actor"; to develop, in my mother's extraordinarily apt and comprehensive phrase, "an unrealistic attitude toward gravity." In bringing myself low, finally, I brought my father to me. I would have a chance—over a year of furious rehabilitation and dangerous illnesses—to show him perseverance, concentration, seriousness. He showed me admiration. The accident defined me as worthy. The more so as it almost killed me.

My father was given the chance to save my life. I had lain in the hospital for a few days, being guarded against death as if I were the Pope, when my lungs became congested. I breathed through mud. I was first put into an oxygen tent, then a respirator, then an iron lung. I was given a tracheotomy. Nothing worked enough. I could not reach the air I pumped for. Without hearing it named, or naming it myself, I was dying.

My father asked the advice of Dr. Alvan Barach, in New York. He knew that Dr. Barach had been working on an automatic "cougher," which, however, was still experimental. An associate of Barach's flew to Burlington with the machine. The machine worked. I'm told that the first mucous it pulled up was so stiff it appeared in the shape of a bronchial tree. The same resident "coughed" me for three days and nights, until I was out of danger.

Friends, relatives, Margaret, began coming to visit and marveled at my spirits. I was cheerful after the crisis. People were evidently too disturbed by the paralysis to see past it, to see that being alive made it easy to be cheerful. The cheerfulness was privately complicated, though, potentially dangerous. Immortality seized me: in exchange for being paralyzed, I would never die. (This exchange seemed for a while to solve a problem that had been terrifying me from early childhood, when I first understood that my life would end someday. But the same terror returned when I got better, and it remains. It is the terror of missing out forever after.) Nor did people know that, on the other hand, I was now convinced that I had cancer, that the accident's results were meant to distract me from my cancer, that everyone knew about my cancer but me. I confided my childlike panic to my mother, made her say, more than once: no, I was not dying of cancer; no medical secrets were being kept from me. The accident had made me so important I would live forever, had so endangered me that just behind the catastrophe a worse catastrophe waited. The imagined cancer must have been a way of minimizing the inescapable actuality of paralysis, of trying to make it disappear through invidious contrast, through the idea of imminent death, make it disappear one way or another.

TWO

WHILE my ancient history has grown familiar to me, only at forty, in my second twentieth year, have I dared begin to scrutinize my history since the accident. Having passed twice, now, that turn in years at which, the first time by, I capsized, and having seen that this time I have made the turn "safely," I am eager (and it finally seems bearable) to review the modern history of the person I have permanently become. I want to re-create my re-creation.

I am frightened, though, as I try to revive the first days in the hospital, by what I don't remember about the time, as if what I don't remember—*because* I don't remember it—will someday, suddenly, spring up and batter me with intolerable news. Tiny pieces of the experience stick to my brain like exploded fragments of skin on a bush. But the same numbness that encased me almost totally from my nipples to the ends of my toes had a mental counterpart, and my recollection of the beginning of my second infancy remains almost totally paralyzed. The moments I do retain are missing their sensations, as if their nerves were mangled. My splotchiness of memory, and the unpalpable nature of the splotches, must be due in part to my mind's distance, at the time, from my body's vanished sensitivity and freedom. I wasn't taking in its disappearance. Memory returns with my body's return.

I don't remember the *sensation* of fighting to breathe, only, vaguely, the ugliness of the iron lung, some glint of sense that it looked to me like a bomb in which I was stuck. (What damage I had done to my world.) And because, in a literal way, I was feeling so little pain, I don't remember how spinal taps, or other, more onerous tests I remember having had, felt. I can remember the sensations of far less disturbing tests given only a few months later. It's as if the faces and events of the first days were seen by one peering from beneath life through a periscope that most of the time was capped.

I was not sedated heavily, I understand. (I ask my brother, a physician, whether I was sedated at all. He tells me yes, probably some. But not heavily? No, he says, that would have interfered with the testing of your recovery. Likely small doses of phenobarbital? Yes. Against nervousness? Nervousness, he says, is not a word that adequately describes what you were going through. I wonder at my underplaying use of "nervousness.")

I lay immobile—except for infantilely wavering arms I moved with a caution that was weakness, and hands curled to frail fists —and almost dead to touch; frozen, preserved for whatever my new life would turn out to be. Was sedation supposed to protect me from assimilation of my state? I still haven't assimilated my state, sedation-free years and states later. About to get out of bed, I sometimes look at the wheelchair into which I am about to slam my ass, and I ask myself what that wheelchair is doing there, parked there. Waiting for whom? If it was principally sedation that blanked out all but a few dots of those early days, I regret the sedation.

Whatever caused it, I resent the amnesia. Not to be able to recall the time vividly makes me feel blind, or, worse, blind-folded. It is not black, the unexpected room of time I lay in—a tiled, science-fictional room with warlike qualities, or a morgue, isolated, gadgeted, as alien as a space can be—but it is darker than dim, a slate-blue, the color of the world after life, or before. The "dark days" are dark. An inconvenient convenience. Doctors, nurses, my mother and father, my brother and his wife, my sister, aunts, uncle, grandmother, a high school friend, Don Rahv, who drove up from New York almost immediately to see what it meant, the news he had heard, were there by the bed, gazing at the new-born child, but I do not recall how they behaved, how they looked, simply the fact of their faces. Only if I had not been me then could I remember me. The pain belonged to those who were not me. I was without pain. I must be saying: I do not want to have been me; I would have preferred the pain and recollections to be mine, the accident someone else's.

The pain of others then is my pain now. My struggle for breath, my period of strictest paralysis, was worst of all, as I gather, for my mother. She tells me that my father had to force her, during the first days, into my room. My mother had always "been there" for me, as much as my father's wife could be, which was more than most mothers with or without tyrannical husbands. I didn't have to bring her to me from nearly as far off as I imagined my father to be. Nor can I imagine—as I seem to feel I imagined being able to do to my father—having driven her away from me by bombing out the family's safety, which my father's heart attacks had merely loosened up. Yet he had to make her go into my room. I had to ask for her. She paced the corridor, not wanting to see me when she didn't know if I would live or die, when she had been told that if I lived it was probable my body would be dead for life. The atmosphere of that corridor my mother paced, resisting my room, is on the verge of terrifying for me to consider. I caused the atmosphere. I aim the rifle of memory at myself: I think of myself, crushed, having crushed my mother, of myself as a disaster who turned the world outside my door gray with ruined relatives.

When I am prompted to imagine closely the initial effect of the accident on either of my parents, my brains and my bones wince, and then they moisten with a sweat of remorse, as if I had sliced a knife through my father's hefty chest, and bashed in the always amazingly soft cheeks of my mother's long-loving face. The man who was Hitler, the woman whom I saw as his powerful slave—no harm they did me, even in my most receptive imagination, has any sensible relation to the punishment I gave them. But neither does my sense of the punishment I gave them have any sensible relation to its actual quality or force. I am able to feel that I didn't know my own strength, as if I did something—to them—too powerfully, too fast, to take back. It is what I am able to feel I did to others that makes me cringe. Shame and vanity merge. The ultimate defensiveness: my injury happened to others. I give it away. Perhaps the intolerable news I fear, like Oedipus, is: I am me.

But if I felt any of this at the beginning, I did not register it and I don't remember it. I do remember, of myself, two flickering spasms of rage in the room's tense, dark dawn. I had a private nurse fired because I thought she was tickling my feet under the oxygen tent, as if I were a baby. And, shortly after my lungs had been cleared, and I was a survivor, I burst out to my mother against a writer named Peter Viereck for an article of his that had infuriated me at the end of my life before. From my shelf, I shouted. (I have a retroactive sense of pleasure that, with my tracheotomy tube covered, I could bellow, and that I could be angry at all.) Also, I remember telling my father, in very subdued alarm, that I was feeling no sexual desire, having no sexual thoughts. He told me this was standard for the situation. A kind of reassurance.

Dreams dictated to my mother a few days to six weeks into my new life take up several pages in the small spiral notebook in front of me, photographs of an infant with a past. I dreamed that my pants were falling down while I, mobile, was being laboriously pursued by a crippled homosexual. I dreamed that some friends freed me from traction so that I could attend high school graduation ceremonies, which took place in the dark in the hospital's basement. At the graduation, I was awarded a sixty-dollar bill and two miniature skeletons. I dreamed that I was supposed to stop a car, occupied by two men, rolling backward down a hill toward me, and that I stepped aside. I dreamed that, wearing leg braces, I walked Margaret to her dormitory. Leaving her, I got caught in a storm and fell down in a field and was unable to rise. In the field I fell asleep. I dreamed that I had to return, to a baby-veterinarian's hospital, a two-year-old boy who had been taking care of me; he had been a bad nurse. I carried him by the ankles because I was mad at him. Some babies in cribs told me he lived in their room, but I didn't want to put him in with the "nice" babies. I carried him into another room and threw him through a trap door into a deep-freeze crib.

Externally, following the decongesting of my lungs, I evidently appeared as follows: screwed into my shaven skull was a skeletal cap of silver bars from which the iron traction ball was suspended; a rubber feeding tube emerged from my nose, the silver tracheotomy tube from my throat, and a catheter poured from my penis into a jar on the floor. My sister-in-law says that on first seeing me in my crib—my bed had side-bars to prevent my falling out during muscle spasms—all this tubing seemed to her irrelevant. There *I* was, so what was all that stuff doing in me? *I* didn't need that. She had as much difficulty taking me in as I did.

I lay throughout the summer in Vermont on an air mattress my father had gotten up from New York, and I was turned, at his insistence, from side to side to my back every few hours, against the possibility of bed sores. His once wearisome, perversely scrupulous regard for safety—for the prevention of abstract danger—seemed to me for the first time a regard for *my* safety and for the prevention of *immediate* danger. The air mattress under me and the rigidly routinized turning of me were a redirected, benign form of his screaming lectures about slamming car doors without looking. Now the nurses were under the gun. In a sense, I lolled on that air mattress, enjoying a victory my paralysis couldn't diminish; my paralysis had caused it. My father's power had turned from ice to water, soothing me as it must have soothed his patients. I moved out of the family, became a patient; he became patient. Did I do him a favor? The father I had typed as a bellowing or irritable immensity was now a sweet, stocky man with a thrice-scarred heart who came up every weekend to see me (and my mother, who was living in a small apartment near the hospital). He lived alone for those summer months. He had been very ill. And that summer, for us, was not to be nearly the worst of it. Yet as much as I cost us in gaining his unqualified love for a time, untying his most curious and supportive interest, didn't I, after all, enable him to show it, free him from the impulse to indulge in domination? What I also forced him to be to me—a doctor—he was famously good at being. Don't parents need to impress their children with their gifts as much as children need to impress their parents with theirs?

The color of my hospital room changes to a glaring yolk-yellow. The late spring and the summer were—misleadingly—joyous. I lived as if in a hammock in a cage suspended in sunlight. Tubes were withdrawn, the silver tracheotomy horn last. (After my throat had been stitched up, I babbled, from the Demerol, and, I like to think, because I had personal, full control of my voice again. No one any longer had to place a finger over the tube when I wanted to talk. The vocal autonomy, the only form I had at the time, made me giddy.) In exhausting twitches, I voluntarily began to move toes and legs. With my weak fists I squeezed rubber balls. A physiotherapist worked me over daily, stretching and pumping the legs, still virtually mute, and the timid-seeming arms. My muscles were being treated as if they had a point to them, as if they were worth trying to save. I might have been in training for a comeback that would start way out of town; still, a comeback. I did not try to conceive where it might take me. I did not visualize my future, I saw only where I had come from and what I was doing now.

The good news I represented—survival, the beginning of recovery—brought people to see me in what seemed a continuously self-renewing supply of congratulation. How far from being cut off I imagined myself to be. The audience was a swarm in the sunlight: friends from Middlebury's theatrico-literary fringe visiting a severed member-thread; students I had barely known; older friends; former teachers on their way through summer Vermont; a deputy from my former summer camp, offering me, to my complex disgust, the job of baseball coach whenever I was up and around; friends of friends; family; Margaret. They flew about my cage. There was a great deal of mail, read to me, the answers dictated by me. (Later, with my mother my secretary, I dictated love letters to Margaret. My mother undertook this job with an absolutely straight face, as if she weren't there, just as she undertook similarly awkward jobs later. Once she revived, she became a pioneer woman.) People telephoned; the receiver was stuck into my fist. I learned that distant novenas were being said for me by people I did not know. Gifts of books and records arrived almost daily, and my father usually carried gifts when he arrived, himself a gift, from New York. I looked forward to these presents, and accepted them, with childlike bluntness. Often people who did not know me well or had not seen me for years, such as my fourth-grade teacher, would ask what I wanted, and I would let them know specifically, down to titles and opus numbers and particular recordings. I had no shame about collecting these consolations, or rewards, or awards. And, in fact, collecting them meant I was vital, if greedy.

Women floated about me in the sunlight, nurses and civilians who became nurses. Staying with my mother in varying combinations were her two sisters and their mother. My grandmother cooked particular dishes for me, brought me wine, read to me Thor Heyerdahl's *Kon-Tiki,* the ultimate travel book. For having been born again, I was indulged like a returning hero, while at the same time, necessarily, I was treated like a physical infant. Infant-hero.

Molly, my morning nurse, attractive, warm, garrulous—from her, in my captivity, I heard the complete plots of many movies I would not have gone near on my feet—fed me breakfast, gave me an enema, then bathed me. As a child, I had brought worms into the kitchen to terrify our housekeeper. Now, with Molly, I clumsily snuck a banana beneath the sheet into my crotch; uncovering me for the bath, she blushed hard, whispering harshly, "Oh, now, you stop that—awful!" in effect, and grabbed away the banana. I sometimes grew real erections as her warm, soapy washcloth stroked me, and her response to them was the same, amused and embarrassed, "mortified." Molly: in her young thirties, happily married, a practicing Catholic, an excellent professional. I: twenty, naked, excited by her hands, unable to use my own hands. If I'd been able to use them on her, I wouldn't have; but if I'd been able to use them at all, she wouldn't have been washing me. The accessibility of my body, the inaccessibility of hers, had implications beyond what is normal in the already peculiar relation of female nurse to male patient. I was a hairy baby being washed, a hairy baby with an adult erection.

It is a small event, but a rich fact to me: during the summer in the hospital, on one of Margaret's visits, I scratched around under her skirt, poking at desire with my stiff fingers. Playing "doctor," getting away with a secret, I was also saying to a Margaret in no position to resist me, to the Margaret who had often resisted going to bed with me behind a locked door: this is what we've come to, playing like kids behind a door anyone can enter without turning a knob or even knocking—it didn't have to be this way. I remember hardly anything else of her visits, and I don't remember where she was when she wasn't visiting me. Far off somewhere. And far off when she was with me. My distance from her shares some of the same cause as the remoteness of the very first, critical, days: my mind's distance from my body's disappearance. Margaret had been the chief purpose of my body's existence for a year, and this body, if it had now begun to return, in steps of inches, with long, peering pauses of uncertainty between, was still well beyond my embrace. I'm sure I felt that Margaret had herself taken my body away, but if I'd known I felt so, I wouldn't have said so. My rage at her before the accident, while usually uncertain, whiny, embarrassed, was always evident. My rage at her after the accident took years to find any breath at all, years even beyond our breaking up, which wouldn't take place for eighteen awkward months. During that time, we were in a boxer's clinch. In the hospital, in fact, Margaret introduced herself to a cousin of mine as my fiancée, a role beyond any understanding we had expressed to each other. (If we were married, we had no need to be engaged.) I'm sure, too, that Margaret must have been enraged with me, for where I had put us. But the outcome of our union—I empty and still— itself made it impossible that we show our rage. *It* was paralyzed. She would have been tactless to show hers, and I, guilty at having put us where we were, was, as well, not ready to think of giving her up if she would stay, not when I needed a woman as proof, in my new life, of my sexuality's previous existence and as an implicit promise of its return.

Margaret and I had first gone to bed together just a little over a year before, at my parents' house, in Westchester, during spring vacation of my freshman year. Poised over her, over the moment I'd been pleading with time for years to make possible, I heard her say, in her dank, diffident way, "Are you quite sure you know what you're doing?"—she meant emotionally, at the moment, not technically—and I, with the hot wind of my passion, answered, in effect, "God! Of course!" And probably, "I love you!" And in I slid, with held breath. Maybe the penis doesn't *know* what to feel at first. When I think of that occasion, occasion of occasions, that answer to years of awed conjecture, I think of sticking a thumb into slush. (A year earlier, with a prostitute, the unofficial first time, had been no less exciting.) Margaret and I lay together for a while, but not long enough. I grew sleepy and got out of bed to return to my room. Margaret stood up on the bed and started climbing onto the windowsill, which was three storeys above an open concrete porch. I dragged her back by the knees. We never became better sexual friends. Much as I admired her brain, and treated it respectfully, my years of groaning frustration in the adolescent waiting room had left me sexually angry and rude once my turn came. For one who, with Margaret, at Middlebury, insisted on associating ardent sex with immaturity, I did not have an adolescence loaded with chances for the sexual expression of ardor.

In the late forties, early fifties, in my group, when a girl said "Don't," most boys quickly said "O.K." I once—just once—put my hand into the pants of my major high school girlfriend. She asked me to remove it, which I did, respectfully; she wept with loving appreciation. Whatever "serious" happened, as a rule, happened at dog speed, with clothes on; "dry-humping." One could sense the hairiness, the soft recess, beneath the skirt, and it seemed all the farther away then. I was continually heavy with mental and physical tumescence; within me wandered a solo Tristan. Tristan with Isolde is already idiot enough. Sexually, in particular, my adolescence made a fool of me, as it had to of most of us. My eyes must have dripped sperm. But when an Isolde would appear, and make herself too clear, I hurried away without looking back.

In the meanwhile, my friends and I, while we went to plenty of ball games and movies, were also going to plays, operas, concerts—grown-up stuff—on our own, from the age of fifteen, and to parties, where, for the most part, what we did with the girls was talk. With great pleasure to ourselves, we pleased, we imitated, our parents. We liked what they liked, and we really did. At fifteen, I was a Thursday evening subscriber to the New York Philharmonic. Little man. We were most favored. Adults smiled upon us. Our entire group was peculiarly unrebellious. We did not get into trouble. It was not difficult being good, grown-up, when we were enjoying ourselves so. Always laughter, on streets, in lobbies, elevators, sudden laughter, clubby laughter, its source a mystery to those not of us; always parody, spontaneous slapstick, practical jokes; always plays, parties. No need for trouble. And in any case, while most of us were without religion, as Ethical Culturized Jews we had conscience to spare.

The Ethical Culture Society, whose school our parents sent us to, was strong on the idea that the better you did by others the better you did for yourself. We were amused even then to recognize that the fathers of many of us couldn't possibly have afforded to send us to Fieldston if they had followed Fieldston's moral plan. The school itself, in fact, paid careful, and often wise, attention to us as individuals. We were fulfilled in most ways. But, wrote Felix Adler, the Society's founder, who had left the rabbinate to start a "religion of duty," "We grow and develop in proportion as we help others to grow and develop." As an adolescent, my private translation of this difficult moral language couldn't have been more clear-cut: penis is pistol. I was not to fire my gun. This was generosity, duty. A genital conceit Felix Adler did not prophesy. It never occurred to me that my female schoolmates, with nothing to fire, were not being generous, or, for that matter, that they might have been suffering, too. After all, why should anyone have been generous to me? It was my duty to be generous to others. Immersed in virtue, and doubled over with desire, I could not see the converse of the Ethical Culture formula. Others existed for me to be good to. The formula had the effect, in high school, of making me a giver, sexually, by not asking or taking.

I graduated from Fieldston sexually voracious, not to say vengeful, and yet, at college, it was Margaret, restrained to the point of coldness, rather than someone hot, tender, or happy, who appeared first as both appropriate and available. Bea, the girl who had rejected me, was appropriate: beautifully morbid-looking, severe, mournful; heavy white skin, long dark hair—a love-death object. And I had rejected another girl, because she seemed stupid and because kissing and touching made her convulsive; she was like boiling water around me. I could not submit. My choice, my necessary choice, of Margaret continues to grieve and infuriate me, even though there is no one to blame for it, even though I have long since outgrown its essential implications of sexual fear and intellectual solemnity. I cannot outgrow the fact of it, or its consequences. As soon as she became my victim, I became hers. My hunger was susceptible to punishment, and she punished it.

During the summer before her junior and my sophomore year at Middlebury, we new lovers separated, Margaret going to South Africa, where her father was managing a ranch, and I to Europe with my friend Don Rahv. (My father surprised me with a camera, my first and last. His generosity made it impossible to refuse the thing. He taught me how to use it, and I used it, but it felt heavy. Heavier still was the contraceptive advice he insisted I get from a colleague of his. More of his damn safety. I felt unable to tell him I didn't need it and wouldn't need it.) On the boat, I read *Ulysses*, wrote poems mocking the first-class passengers, and compiled letters of observation and longing to mail to Margaret. Much of the rest of the time, Rahv tried to persuade me to "have fun" when we reached Paris. We expressed ourselves vertically each night in our double-decker bunks. Rahv would say down to me: you're only young once, enjoy yourself, for God's sake. The Louvre isn't everything. This is our chance! I said up to him: I will remain loyal to Margaret. When you are in love for good, loyalty is inevitable. I extolled her, hoping to convince him.

Once in Paris, I gave in almost instantly. But carefully, I imagined. The second or third night, I spotted a plain, chubby whore easily fifty years old (or so she seemed to me then), who, when I nodded to her, signaled to me to follow. We ended up in a room in a tiny hotel. She kept her black garter belt on and I kept my socks on, my francs tucked in one of them, and we had a quick lay. She cried out compliments to me in simple French. I met Rahv downstairs, and he congratulated me. Later that night, I wrote to Margaret a cheerful letter explaining how, in doing the merely obligatory thing, I had chosen myself such a bag as to deny myself pleasure for the sake of our relationship. I didn't hear from Margaret for the rest of the trip. The next night I watched Rahv go off with a whore killingly young and beautiful.

After we had spent three weeks companionably in and around Paris, Rahv left for the Riviera and I for England. (On the Channel boat, I encountered the doctor who had dispensed the contraceptive information. Had my father hired him to follow me, to make sure I was taking pictures and protecting myself? We spent the rough trip to Dover balancing, smiling, spasmodically comparing travel notes.) In London, I met with a few people I knew from the States, or was supposed to look up, but I was mostly alone, and staying alone in a borrowed apartment in a dead outskirt. As Margaret continued to send me cold silence from Africa, I shriveled into misery. Finally, I tried telephoning her, but the ranch was beyond the phone's reach.

Toward the end of my stay, increasingly numb, I managed to get a ticket for the closing performance of *Much Ado About Nothing*, John Gielgud as Benedick, Diana Wynyard as Beatrice. The numbness melted. I was embraced by the play's, and the production's, perfection: sustained confidence—I'd never seen anything so complex that seemed to know so fully and easily what it was doing—jauntiness, wit, color, grace, charm, *smartness*; it was a beautifully bright microcosm spinning evenly before me, a brilliant human garden. And my chest slumped at the ending, in which the two smart alecks who love each other confess their love and allow it to draw them, at last, together. And there I was, at the curtain, cheering, and then, out on the street, in the blackness and lights, alone again, now naked and in a panic.

I fled to Hyde Park, where, I'd heard, whores could be found. They were said to do their fucking standing up so that they could make quick recoveries if bobbies came by. It's not that the idea of the position appealed to me particularly. My loneliness and anger were so overwhelming that the position seemed beside the point. Sure enough, the women were there, glinting in the black greenery like whitewashed hitching posts. I approached one. Half a pound, she said. I gave her half a pound. She lowered her pants, lifted her skirt. I lowered my pants. I needn't have bothered. My penis was as limp as braised celery, and it stayed limp no matter how much rubbing or repositioning we did. I pulled up my pants and rushed off to find another dim whore, whom I paid another half a pound, out of my anxious budget, with the same result. I went home to the apartment in the dismal suburb feeling ridiculous, jumpy, embarrassed, as if my misery had been carbonated and were now giddy. I wrote to Margaret, as, shouting pleas, complaints, and demands into her frightening silence, I had been continuing to do. She could have been critically ill with some African disease as well as angry. I described the *Much Ado,* but I refrained from dramatizing my loneliness with the scene in Hyde Park. I'm sure I was tempted to tell her. Good stories don't come along that often, and I liked to *share* everything with her. When I arrived back in America, I found a letter waiting for me at my father's office, the tiny, exquisite grass of Margaret's hand crushed here and there by pale coins of tears, the money she had laid out to pay for my frivolity and insensitiveness. I remained in debt.

At Middlebury in the fall of 1952, Mike and I moved into our basement apartment, and Margaret and I resumed our "marriage," against the odds of our inexperience, her curfew, her fear of talk (in 1952, sex at college was a punishable offense), my swing-from-the-heels lust, her resistance to it, condoms bursting with deadly semen, delayed menstrual periods, her delayed reports of their ultimate arrival. This was sex at last. Blanched, I would walk around for days, carefully, trying not to disturb the Goddess of Menstruation, who made her decisions just beneath my feet. I did not want marriage with my marriage. Once, crunched by worry, I went to see a biology instructor on behalf of the cliché friend who has a problem and asked him to explain ovulation to me, my over-anxious questions strangling his answers, so that I failed to understand them well. Then I took his answers home and tried to jibe them with significant dates I couldn't be sure were accurate. All that sloppy, crucial addition and subtraction, and the varying answers to the problem worthless on their own.

I wore a black suit of maturity many sizes too big, in which I flapped around as if I thought it fit. Having regular sex at all, and in an apartment rather than a car or a field, was mature; participating in campus life from its isolated artist's corner was mature; Margaret was mature: British-born and British-spoken, superior to me in age, familiar with great *obscure* works by trustworthily great composers and writers; she took Russian; for an art course, she constructed a replica of a Persian temple—*she* did it with *her* hands, *my* girlfriend—and its complex delicacy amazed everyone; I was not left alone to praise it and doubt what I was praising for lack of company. She choreographed a ballet for herself, composed a serial sonata for guitar and recorder, wrote difficult, formally sensitive poems, and stories based on myths. I saw Margaret as peculiar and sober, the ideal combination for me; I fought away infections of cliché coming from any direction, and I badly needed to feel that art was responsible—much of "responsible" meaning, at that time in my life, completed. If a serious work was finished, it almost had to be good. It was, then, not an effort to prove oneself, but proof of oneself. Such proof equaled excellence.

To persuade my parents that I was a good enough poet not to be wasting my time or my future, I praised my own work as I mailed it to them. To persuade them that poetry itself was worthwhile (a key word of my childhood), I once wrote, from college: "Perhaps the most distinguishing mark between contemporary and past poetry is the use the poet makes, today, of a poem for other purposes than a blithe command to Corrina that we go 'a-Maying.' . . . Poetry has come to embody a more intellectual approach; it is, of course, no longer an art, or pastime, designated only to a leisure class; it is no longer a foppery. Nor is this to say that it always was—of course not, but it is now used to say much, much more about many, many more things than it has been at various stages of growth . . . poetry has become more intellectual and, thereby, perhaps, more valuable or useful." As a sophomore, I read, in Henry James's "The Art of Fiction," "One perceives . . .—by the light of a heavenly ray—that the province of art is all life, all feeling, all observation, all vision," and this announcement, from an entrenched divinity, was a heavenly ray to me. I remember, in fact, being surrounded by sunlight when the passage appeared before my eyes, and feeling, in the warmth of the sun and of the reconciling but perfectly obvious words, that I had been touched by revelation, and that my future had been justified.

The oversized black suit I wore in imitation of maturity and out of panic over my father's health gave me freedom, but only for a while, to grab for support without ripping its seams. Almost everybody imitates as a youth—as I imitated literary and sexual adulthood, ignorant of craft in either—until one can finally *be*. What I first finally became was a survivor, following the accident. People rarely imitate survival. I cannot separate my youthful pretenses from my abrupt arrival at realities so huge and immediate that I was unable even to try transcending them by imitating them. The imagined maturity of my relationship with Margaret couldn't, after all, contain our immaturity. We asked the impossible, and the unnecessary, of each other. Everything we did we could have done without pretending we were accomplished or experienced. Sexually, we slapped at one another for a year, not seeing that we had reached the edge of a cliff. I gave the final—and only literal—slap, the one she requested, remorseful over some obstinacy or retaliation, on the May afternoon in 1953. I gave it feebly, no less to blame than she for the sexual feud we couldn't stop. And the next afternoon it was I who fell over. I traded imaginary adulthood for physical infancy.

My concern for the future that summer was only immediate, the scope of my imagination as limited as the range of my legs' movements. I feared nothing, looked forward to nothing specific. The present occupied almost all my mind. The present was a present: a prolonged surprise party in the cage suspended high in the glaring yolk-yellow sunlight. What I could do physically was all victory, progress away from death or stasis. What I couldn't do—walk, feed myself, write, turn over in bed, move my bowels voluntarily, control my urination significantly, bathe myself—I didn't mind, and may even have liked, not doing. In an isolated hospital room it was easy enough to get used to. In any case, because movement had started to return, I knew that everything necessary would return. I didn't define "necessary." I assumed the eventual arrival of an unimagined self-sufficiency. So, when I was visited one day by a former Middlebury student —an ex-officio member of my fringe—and she introduced me to the man she was with as "Dick Brickner, who cracked up in a car and has ruined himself for good," her stunning words became an anecdote with which I could regale my admiring guests, watching them share my hilarious amazement, the amazement standing at the same time for the thrilling flashiness of her bad taste and for her so obvious inaccuracy.

She was wrong. But I remember her remark, having forgotten many other stunners, because, at the time she made it, I knew absolutely nothing about my future; I couldn't, and didn't want to, but I assumed I did. Her confidence that I had ruined myself for good, though ugly, reminds me of my own naïveté, balances it. I would not begin to know anything until the cage had been lowered and I removed from it. And what I discovered was often disturbing and dangerous. Some of the future moved backward almost to the beginning again. It held sudden, jarring drops, detours, tunnels, and dead ends. I dislike, from that time, as I dislike from my earlier life, my expectation of unearned accomplishment. One of the benefits of my future was to be the luxury of having passed, after much negotiation, critical tests, and the development, with success, of a love for emotional earning. The luxury feels similar to having a fat wallet. The feeling

MY SECOND TWENTY YEARS

has the same capacity to mislead, but it's a peculiarly good feeling to have when it's around.

The sun of the summer receded. I was lowered, in soft jolts, to the ground. With the traction ball detached, I sat on the bed's edge, supported by at least two people, dizzy, sweating, boneless, the bed a tiny ledge, the floor three feet below me a sidewalk thirty feet away. A day or so later, an orderly swung me from the bed into an armchair. In mid-September, the traction bars still sticking from my skull but the iron ball left behind, I was slid into a hearse-ambulance and driven, on my back, to New York, to the Institute of Rehabilitation Medicine, popularly known as the Rusk Institute. Molly accompanied me. When we reached the Institute, the black car poured down a ramp into urban dimness, what seemed like a concrete pit, where the sun reached grayly. Somehow I knew that pasted to the windshield of the hearse-ambulance was a sticker reading "Invalid Car." I asked Molly to have the sticker removed before the Institute attendants saw it. She said no.

THREE

I SEE MYSELF as fractured, for the first time, at the Institute. My memories of myself there flash on broken glass, sharp to hold. I see myself as fractured because, once I'd been brought down from the cage of my hospital room, I was naked, my weaknesses were naked. I was now in the cellar beneath the world. The others in the cellar with me told me by how they appeared how I appeared.

I remember myself as dismembered, fractured in the most complete possible sense, and as if I were waiting to be repaired, for limbs and head to be rejoined to torso, and as if, once I were reunited with myself, my nakedness would be covered. At the Institute I was, for the first time, ashamed. The Institute did nothing to cover me.

I am being fed by a female aide. She refers to me, in conversation with a passing colleague, as a "quad," for quadriplegic. "He's a quad." I say to her that this is not so, knowing she will not understand, or possibly not believe me, if I explain that I am quadriparetic, weak in all limbs, not paralyzed. (She can't mean "quad" for quadriparetic. Quadriparetic is an obscure term and quadriparesis an uncommon condition.) In any case, her manner of reference sets the tone of the place for me. We, the patients, are he, she, quads (and paras? amps?). A science-fiction language. New world; new life. I felt as if, because of their physical superiority, the aides were unhappy to help me. I felt ruled by slaves.

My friend Charnas comes to visit me. Charnas, who had been the essence, in high school, of our alert giddiness, our improvised prepolitical street theater, our genteel juvenile delinquency, our boisterous mockery and self-mockery. We improvised as if we had rehearsed. Everything clicked, or seemed to, or now seems to have. We sang loudly on the busiest streets, choruses from Gilbert and Sullivan or songs from Marx Brothers movies. We limped imaginatively (I was once heaving, in a new style, along Broadway, my cronies observing from behind, when I saw a real limper—though it's possible he was faking, too, imitating me—coming toward me in the same style. Of course, under the circumstances, I couldn't stop my heavily unbalanced rocking motion. I continued past him, feigning concentration on my progress. The show must go on). We begged on street corners for funds to cure our syphilis; we wore horrible masks for scaring old ladies; in packs we snuck into the second acts of Broadway shows; we dueled with butter knives in the Automat; we wrote maniacal plays, every line hilarious to us, in homage to the combined techniques of Perelman and Benchley (who had come to fame in our parents' youth). We formed a Rabelais Society—Rabelais, honored scatologist, the ideal writer for pleasing our silliness while confirming our erudition—and a Latinist among us drew up a list of ornate titles for the Society's officers. We filmed a slapstick *Medea*, I the Medea, glowering, in heavy lipstick, writhing along the floor, a monster of vengeance, in a white sheet with a tail of neckties. Undergraduate intellectual stuff, "precocious." And obnoxious, no doubt, but not to us. We were always in theatrical motion, and Charnas, who when serious was loving, and very shy, easily embarrassed, led us in gusto. There was a maturity, even if naïve, in the satirical silliness of our high school days that for me had vanished as I hurried, at college, on a campus of childish collegians, into my satirizable solemnity. Now I lay, coming to, on the bank of my own evolution. And here was Charnas, visiting me from enviable Harvard, at his most shy and loving, but bearing a reminder of our distant yet recent anarchism: a large dill pickle. He handed it to me, he remembers, from its paper bag, and I was unable to hold onto it. I don't remember the dill pickle. What I remember is that, when Charnas came in, I was in the midst of a high colonic enema, on a bedpan but fully covered by bedding. During Charnas's visit, the orderly overseeing my enema came by to see how I was doing and without a word of warning ripped the bedding off me.

I am examined by the doctors at the Institute, after which the staff social worker tells me and my parents that I should plan for a career as a lens-grinder.

I was evidently not to expect to return to college, not to expect to use myself in a personal way. I remember reacting with scorn: however my capabilities were going to develop, or fail to develop, I was not going to be anything like a lens-grinder. (Scorn was easy.) The crudity of the Institute's vocational prognosis, the implicit pessimism of the physical prognosis, so upset and puzzled my parents that my father, desperate, called on his friend David Gurewitsch, an esteemed doctor of physical (rehabilitation) medicine. Gurewitsch came to see me. He seems, in memory, to have simply appeared at my bedside. It was like a stage entrance made in the dark. His presence had the kind of impact that tightens life into a scene. I remember his tall calmness filling my vision, and his physical beauty. The calm was in his bearing, pace, and voice; his eyes were excited. Insofar as it is possible to say so, he didn't have a doctor's face; he had an artist's face but a doctor's kind of poise. He examined me and talked with me. And then he told my parents that I would be able to do with my life what I wanted to do with it.

For years afterward, when I went to see him, he congratulated himself and me on the accuracy of his original conviction that I would have a large hand in my own life, that my will would not be wasted. I would leave his office feeling as if I were a victory, more valuable to the world than a victor. With his death, early in 1974, I gaze after him. Though I had less to do with him than with others who had been and were to be crucially helpful, he couldn't help but be my chief guide over the longest stretch of my recovery. He had been able to say: you have a future to create; accident will not win. I followed his conviction. Yet, it was my father who brought Gurewitsch to me.

It would be a long while, though, before his conviction made sense. My last memory of myself at the Institute is that I am tipping again toward death, as if the bed were being tilted backward and I were slipping off it. The blood in my head is drying. My breath is floating out of reach. My lungs are too short; they strain and strain at air and come up with nearly nothing. The trouble is that my bladder, still sluggish from the accident's effects, had needed help, and I had been catheterized. Now my bladder is infected. I am being lined with icepacks. My temperature—I learn this from an aide, whom I ask, who tells me with an impressed grin—is 105 degrees. I am just as I was with Mike on the road, in a tantrum of panic. The nurse lacks Mike's control, and in her panic berates me for mine. She might have been saying: you are not supposed to die on us; this is a place of rehabilitation. The next day, when my fever has been brought down some, I escape in an ambulance to a hospital.

Five months after the accident, I arrived home. In the same October of the previous life, I would have been in Middlebury again. I felt more exposed at my parents' than I had at the Institute. Our old dining room table had been disassembled and moved into the cellar. In its place, a hospital bed, with sidebars, had been installed. The dining room, on the ground floor, was larger and more accessible than my old bedroom on the third floor, next to the one Margaret had slept in a year and a half before. My family ate in the adjacent kitchen or in the living room upstairs. A male nurse fed me, gave me an enema, bathed me, slept in the room with me. I was a passive invader, unfamiliar with myself, unfamiliar within the familiar walls.

Whatever I did showed me as weak, and there were no signs forthcoming of further muscular recovery. Each morning I was slid onto a "tilt-board" and strapped into it. The board would be swung vertically to the floor, dragged to the wall by the male nurse, and tipped against it. I half stood, half hung there, faint, sweating, drooping, hoping to save my bones. Late mornings, I sat out on the porch, in my first wheelchair. The fall sun burned firmly; I blinked. The sky was a wide-open deep blue. Everything, sun, sky, the garden, was full-bodied, sharply defined. I felt particularly dazed, an old man, in the atmosphere of the gorgeous days that must have been, for others, huge trumpets blown by them. I felt separated from nature. I was, in fact, living my essential childhood fear of missing out forever after. I was sitting up in a glass coffin.

At my father's request, a friend of his, an engineer, developed for me an electric hand, a wired glove operated by a large box with buttons on it. It served me no better than my own fingers. In the *Daily News* there appeared an article to the effect that I, once depressed and dependent, was now, thanks to the miracle of the electric hand, renewed. The misrepresentation scalded me, confirmed my helplessness. The article and my anger were beside the point to my innovative father; the point for him was that the hand, for all he and the engineer knew, could still be improved on. But I didn't care that the hand did not work or that it might be improvable. I did not want that hand.

It was brought home to me and my parents that I was a problem—no longer the success of the first few months—and proven to be dangerous in my physical frailty. I must have suggested to all of us what the saddest possible future for our home would be, a future that would darken us and the house, that would identify it to passing children as ominous and to adults as the nice yellow stucco with the tragic young man downstairs.

And I was it, the tragedy, the pathetic body, the unpleasant mystery. I would be unable to bear the people willing to visit me.

I was ashamed. But I could not have acknowledged shame at the time. To say, or show, that I was ashamed would have seemed to name me as shameful for good. My terror of the possibility I possessed—of remaining what I had become—made the possibility impossible to imagine; and it's as if it made the possibility impossible. "You never think it's going to happen to you." When it happened to me, the bottom three-quarters of my brain didn't think it had happened. I must have thought: if I think it has happened, it will stay happened.

After a month or so at home, I was again having trouble—now more distinct—urinating. And while I sweated out the dry moments, long metal teeth clenched in the meat at the back of my brain, a pain so concentrated I imagine it now as having been potentially lethal in itself. I returned to the hospital downtown, where it was discovered that I had a urethral stricture, scar tissue. The stricture is the accident's accident.

In the hospital, I underwent a urethral dilatation: a gently curved, nickel-plated rod, known as a "sound," a little less than a foot long, its width chosen for the tightness of the stricture but reaching approximately the fatness of a fountain pen, is inserted into the urethra and pushed along until it has been worked past the stricture's tough growth, forcing it to recede. The pain is the pain of ultimate pressure. The penis is suffocated. When the sound enters, my body tightens, and I start to writhe and to breathe panically. The experience confuses exit and entrance, maleness with femaleness, sex with castration. Yet the procedure is brief and not likely to be dangerous.

I stayed in the hospital awhile, since I was going to be dilated at short intervals, with sounds of increasing size; I was also having some neurological tests. In the hospital—a place of transience (one way or another), not at home, where I could have died of helplessness, been "taken care of"—at lunch one day I fed myself, for the first time in over five months. Time had been teaching my nerves. The fine kind of instinct that tells us before explicit symptoms appear that we are sick told me my hands were ready to be active. I heard my nerves waiting. I picked up a fork and, as a child would, used it. The act was too familiar, still, for its return to be dramatically exciting.

That same afternoon, I "wrote" with a pencil. In the same mysteriously accurate way I had sensed I should pick up the fork, and then the pencil, I knew, once I had begun to use them, that the maneuvers of feeding would eventually become complex and refined again, and that the huge letters of unpredictable shape I drew at first would tighten into normal script. But I am sensitive to evidence of my original clumsiness. If I find in my library a book I wrote my name in when my hand was still unfirm, I tear out the inscribed page and write my name new, on the next page. If my hand is fatigued, today, my writing may jump or cramp. I have retyped long letters solely because I felt I must do my signature over.

One afternoon, I left the hospital for my first movie since the accident—the film about Gilbert and Sullivan, starring Robert Morley and Maurice Evans—in a large taxi, with my parents and the male nurse. I sat in the taxi, in the wheelchair, like a carton. Our family had, for years, shared pleasure in the Gilbert and Sullivan operettas, through many performances and through my father's old recordings. There was, especially between my father and my brother and me, a subtle reciprocity of pleasure. My father saw that we loved what he had loved from about the same age as we were now. He could take comfort in the safe passage of the operettas from his youth to ours—they had not died of scorn; on the contrary. He, and my brother and I, fully approved the other generation's enthusiasm. Gilbert and Sullivan, of all things, equalized us. Going to the movie now suggested restoration of several kinds: the past, health, mutuality.

The urologist in charge of me at the hospital protested my

going to the movie—the cold November, a chance of reinfection —but my father carried out his disagreement with the doctor. A few days later, I left the hospital for home again. There, imaginatively and crucially, my father decided that I must return to the hospital in Burlington, where I would continue the urethral treatments and do my basic physical rehabilitation. The staff, outstanding at all levels, and working in a relatively small institution, would give me the efficient, thorough, and coordinated attention it had been impossible to get in New York. In New York, an orderly, pushing me on a stretcher through the hospital's enormously long basement corridor, had let go of the stretcher to watch it sail around a corner, and it had crashed into the wall.

I wanted, as if it were the final thing I would have a chance to do on earth, to go to a Toscanini concert being given at Carnegie Hall the night before I left for Vermont: the NBC orchestra playing Beethoven's *Eroica* symphony. Some friends, at my probably exploitive request, managed to wangle two of the rare tickets. My mother and I went. The disapproving male nurse lifted me into an aisle seat. He waited outside during the concert, a body-chauffeur. It was his last night with us. The performance did not have the intensity I'd anticipated. I was feeling like a piece of crumbled pound cake. The evening summarizes the confusing period: pathetic but promising; I clumsily wrestling my paralysis. I had gained a child's violent will: I would not stay a child.

My mother and I flew to Burlington. I dribbled urine. Dr. Donaghy and an ambulance met us at the airport. I was put in my original room, at the end of the corridor. My mother flew home.

Until I turned boulevardier, at sixteen, I had been successful at sports. In my early adolescence I was an athletic leader among my schoolmates. My "unrealistic attitude toward gravity" did not apply when I was tumbling, catching passes, batting, shooting baskets. I suspect that my instinct for imitation had a lot to do with my athletic ability (and a lust for drama, the intense and crucial), but these qualities don't explain fully why my body, so careless at other times, became effectively obedient to the laws of sports. I was not merely an imitator, but natively adept.

When I lost interest in sports—too small and slow for varsity distinction, wanting to smoke, not wanting to practice—disdain for the physical set in. By the time I reached college, I was classically scornful of athletes, athletics, and exercise. I wore sneakers with large holes in them.

I spent my junior year at Middlebury an hour's drive north of it, trying to learn to walk. First steps: between parallel bars, helped to my feet by one of the physiotherapists, my body braced rigid by my own bones, my arms trembling, the therapist behind me pushing the wheelchair, which would catch my body like a bucket in case it buckled. I marched, on shaking legs, with a slowness that has no measurement in music, for perhaps ten feet, and collapsed, sweating, into the chair. After a rest, as exhausted as one would normally be from trekking miles in too much sun, I "walked" back to the other end of the bars, and collapsed again. A grim, doddering athlete, age one, age twenty, age ninety, I struggled through this exercise not because I was expected to walk to work in the future, but because who knew?, and because the physiotherapists were putting great care into me (for physiotherapists, exercise is what dental hygiene is to dental hygienists—absolutely everything), and because I was there to strengthen my body to its limits. I had no choice. I had no choices. I needed choices.

At Christmas-time, a professor of music at Middlebury came to visit me in the hospital. I had done very well in Alan Carter's course, liked the man, loved the man's subject. Carter was a sophisticated spirit, he told anecdotes about musical eminences, had married the daughter of a famous artist, and so became for me alluring, someone who made me eager to show I knew what he was talking about. At Middlebury, I was one of very few with that capability. Carter stood for the life I wanted to enter from college as a full-fledged member, a figure of glamorous artistic accomplishment.

His visit did me particular honor at a time when it was unclear whether I would be entering the world again at all. Carter had a handsomely round face, distinguished and cocky, the kind that looks good beneath a homburg; his cheeks were the subtle pink of expensive drapes, his jacket heathery. You knew he made good martinis, this man. His presence in my hospital room was like an expensive gift. We chatted about Middlebury and New York, the places of my former precocity. I brought him up to date on my progress, proud of it, telling him I would belong again, impressing him: to say I could now feed myself, was getting stronger, was walking at the parallel bars, to speak optimistically, was to impress.

An orderly interrupted to tell me I was wanted downstairs in the physiotherapy room. But I had a visitor, I pointed out. I asked the orderly to go to the nurse's desk and call downstairs to find out what was going on. When he came back, he reported that he had been told to tell me I would find out what was going on when I got downstairs, and that I must go now.

Carter left, I apologizing in fury. The orderly helped me to dress, guided me into my wheelchair, pushed me down the corridor and into the elevator.

In the physiotherapy room, the rehabilitating patients, on stretchers and in wheelchairs, were arranged in a semicircle. I was wheeled in among them, all of us feeble, some drooping, with age, disease, stroke, or injury; babies, youths, the senile. The patients were spooning or being fed a pale pink ice cream. A visitor, whom I recognized as the wife of the Drama Director down at Middlebury, was standing behind a table, demonstrating how to make Christmas-tree ornaments out of a malleable metal. She braided and otherwise bent the metal into a variety of shapes.

Afterward, I expressed my rage, weeping without tears, to a

huge gung-ho therapist, imperious with the virtue of her profession. She gave my rage right back to me: was I too good for them? It had been a Christmas party, for all of us, from the Physiotherapy Department.

By springtime I was able to cover, with a struggling shuffle, the entire length of the corridor upstairs—the same one my mother had paced almost a year before—gripping a four-legged metal support called a walker—and enter the same room my mother had feared to enter—and fall into bed. But each night, I saturated the sheet with urine, asleep too deeply to reach for the urinal I kept by me. I rang for the floor nurse. I washed myself; she changed the bedding.

When my mother came to bring me home, in April, I was healthy. My urethra worked. I could feed and wash myself. Lying down, I could dress myself. I could get myself in and out of my wheelchair. I had a useful degree of urinary retention. I needed an enema, still, to move my bowels. I was off to visit Margaret.

FOUR

ARGARET had transferred from Middlebury to Clark University in Massachusetts to study the science of cartography. In its demand for the precise rendering of tiny detail, cartography was the ideal function for Margaret. She liked to stand out, in whatever she did, through diminutiveness. She was contractive, not expansive. And it was important to her—and to me—that whatever she did should be "serious" while it was peculiar. As she refined herself, Margaret was sustaining the chief reason for my original interest in her.

Over summer vacation, she came down to join her mother, Doris, at an operatically massive mansion in Connecticut that served for most of the year as a private school. Doris, having left her husband, and up against it financially, had taken the job of caring for the badly crippled child of the school's headmaster. At the beginning of June, my mother drove me up to the estate, where I spent the month, paying board to eat with Margaret, Doris, and the headmaster and his family in the family's apartment in one wing of the mansion, and sleeping, at the other end of a corridor as fat as a subway tunnel, in a vast room that must have held thirty beds during the school year. Margaret slept next door to me. The people in the apartment must have assumed that I would no more be screwing with Margaret than their crippled child would be or else they didn't care. Did any of them happen to tune accurately into our fuzzy station?

I was halfway back in life, half-unwrapped, half out of the box, parts of me dangling over the edges. An awkward position for engaging with full reality, even if full reality—Margaret and I, one year after, at a sexual reunion in a deserted dormitory room in a palace in Connecticut—was as awkward. Where people get to! It was a situation in a dream, or from the film of a director who matter-of-factly, with an "original vision" that is, in fact, accuracy itself, shows how unconventional reality is. Margaret had a job as a waitress in the local town. Each night, when she returned, she would take down her platinum hair and take off her lime-green uniform, and come into my bed. She thought herself to be, she had told me, in the process of sexual awakening. This news was ironic to the point of malice. If Margaret was going through a sexual awakening, I had no way of finding out, and so she had no way of showing me. My penis dozed through all our commotion of effort. We worked out every night like commandos in training. But my skin, her skin, felt to me like rubber, and my brain—I of course kept this to myself —was only trying to feel.

It may be that I was showing Margaret passive resistance, not neurological failure. It is unlikely for the time, but yet not far-fetched, that I was "choosing" to refuse the Margaret who had punished me with her own resistance, as I had punished her with my lust, from the beginning—the Margaret on the window-sill; the Margaret of the unannounced menstrual periods; the Margaret to whom I had vowed such artificially adult fidelity, and whom I had so juvenilely betrayed; the Margaret who had tortured me with silence from inaccessible Africa; the Margaret who had sent me to Hyde Park, where I had been sexually as stymied standing up as I was now lying down; the Margaret whose last act of resistance in my previous life, as I have often supposed, made me so angry that I stepped on the clutch instead of the brake; and the Margaret now undergoing her vengefully timed sexual "awakening."

I returned to my parents' with my resistance pressing on my

brain, and it remained persistently uncomfortable during the summer and through the fall. I couldn't absorb what I couldn't understand. It wasn't supposed to be there, this disloyal doubt, but then why did it sit there, every day, behind my eyes? I couldn't discuss it with Margaret or with my parents. To do so would have been like confessing a sin, I felt. We were miserable, certainly; but maybe misery was what love became for everyone; maybe I was only learning what everyone learned as love lasted. If this was the case, why start over with someone else? (And with whom?) It was instinct that educated my inexperience. By January, it had declared to me that love could not mean a frozen twilight, an afterdeath. I wrote to Margaret—we were corresponding, I in my crude new hand, she in her impeccable lawn of a script—and her reply did not argue with me. We had not argued out loud since the accident. I told my parents what I had done, feeling as if I had let them down. They did not seem to feel as if I had let them down.

A few years later, after Margaret had married, she wrote to me. I answered, the relationship evidently not yet finished. We wrote, very occasionally, for perhaps six years, until, in a letter following a visit she paid me, she accused me of being unfriendly. I only needed her to tell me I was unfriendly to be so; it amounted to permission, if not a request. I sent her a furious reply that slammed the door and locked it.

It is somewhat as if we had been each other's parents, had created each other; having made an increasingly bad job of it, we finally turned away for good. The accident happened to both of us.

In May, before my mother had driven me up to my second honeymoon with Margaret, my mother had driven me down to Columbia University for an interview with the Admissions Director. My grades at Middlebury had been good enough to make me academically acceptable to Columbia College, but the Director was concerned whether I could endure the required schedule. Not, as I remember, whether I could take care of myself in a dormitory. (I must have felt I'd be able to, "somehow.") The intelligent but disappointing decision was that I should delay entering the College for a year, while taking two courses a semester at Columbia's School of General Studies, gaining credits against the College's requirements and extending my endurance gradually. My mother would drive me in twice a week.

I had, by now, enough energy and—simply by being able to get in and out of my wheelchair by myself, and to wheel it—enough flexibility to make me impatient at the idea of living at home for a year and more. Nine months before, in the dining room, my body had been its own lock and key. Freedom had been imperative, but escape inconceivable. Now, in limbo, I was lively enough to feel myself imprisoned. I no longer had the invading invalid's power, retinue of attention, equipment. Crisis and celebrity had fallen away from me. My presence weighed much less. I was, finally, starting from bottom. Living at the bottom of the house, I felt squelched—by the height of the house, the problematic stairs, footsteps above me.

People could now begin to be an interference. My mother's mother—who the year before had traveled by train, alone, from her house up to the devastation in Burlington, to give support to her daughter and to help keep me company—had since come to live with us, age seventy-seven. She had been a particularly forceful, adventurous woman; she was now jittery with painful bone decalcification. My grandmother had a great tolerance for tragedy—it couldn't, on the whole, have surprised her less—but almost none for physical pain. I remembered her as making color all around her, a great gardener of flowers and vegetables, an expert sewer and knitter, an amateur painter; now her gusto had been replaced by general apprehension. Her directorial nature, which she had used to its best advantage as a leader of the earliest child-study group in America, remained, but without point.

When I was nine, spending the summer at my grandparents'

house in Connecticut, I would sit in the hayloft of the barn, smoking Wings cigarettes I'd stolen from my grandmother, and, from my hidden bleacher seat, watching the family play croquet. Toward the end of the summer, my grandmother privately and quietly confronted me with the hired man's report of a pile of butts found beneath the hay. Fire and gravity I treated with the same disrespect. My grandmother's scolding was the most beautiful a child can have; its nature impressed me so much that its substance impressed me equally. In adolescence, when I began leaning away from what I felt to be her self-importance and dogmatism, and toward my theater-loving grandfather, I retained gratitude for the wisdom and tact of the woman who had called me out of the dining room in Connecticut with her shaming discovery.

At the bottom of the house, I could not tolerate my grandmother, did not try to redeem her with recent or older memories, could not afford to sympathize. She drifted down from my old bedroom on the third floor to be with me, lonely (or watchful? An enfeebled nurse?), my parents at work on the second floor. I was at work, too, having started to write stories, but that was merely writing, not my mother's patients, or the elaborate research my father was completing in his enforced retirement from practice. I sat at a long table, facing the garden. My grandmother sat across the room, behind me, sleeping in an armchair, or smoking. I do not remember her trying to make conversation. But my neck felt her as if she were breathing on it. I couldn't say or do anything about these silent visits that made so much noise in me. I sulked. At dinner, on the porch, did anyone want beer? Yes, I did. No, my grandmother didn't; she would "just have a sip" of mine. Each of those sips, at that time, drank a pint of blood from me. I could conceive of no way to protest that would not show me as petty. A mutual friend of Margaret's and mine from Middlebury, Jane, came to see me. We sat out on the porch, in the dark. I felt a miraculous-seeming sexual breeze start up in me. Nervously, I tried to formulate the repercussions of kissing Jane; would she feel awkward because I was still involved with Margaret; because people were nearby indoors; because she would have to respond, whether she wished to or not, if she weren't to appear insensitive? Or would she be receptive? If she were receptive, would it be worth it? I didn't have a chance to decide, no less put my lips on Jane's. My grandmother opened the French doors. It was time to come in, she said, it was getting late now.

My grandmother had nothing to do but me. I was food for the feeble, appropriate to her needs and tired abilities, her counterpart; and yet, her nine-year-old son; and yet, twenty-one years old.

My daily life since the turn of the year had featured women devoted to "bringing me up," or serving my remaining infant-like needs. My existence was staffed by "nurses," not merely the floor nurses in Burlington, but the two physiotherapists, and, later, Margaret, my mother, my grandmother, and our house-keeper, who bore my bedpan from the dining room as matter-of-factly as if it were an unfinished plate. My father was essentially "upstairs." He complained that the odor of my bedpanned bowel movements floated up to him (I do not know that he was right; my mother explained to me that he'd always had a shit phobia; but I didn't *belong* in the dining room, he reminded me, whether he was right or not), and at dinner he would point out, distressed, that I was cutting my tomato into pieces too large for healthy or polite eating. Was it because I found cutting difficult? he wondered, with his scientist's seriousness, complicating my self-consciousness. He would observe, too, that I used my hands gracefully. He behaved toward me again about as he had before the accident, with the same proportion of busy impatience to loving regard, but my dependence on women rattled me more than he could. I didn't depend on him. He did not, in a literal way, surround me.

During July, my mother drove me downtown a number of times for exercise and functional training (shirt-buttoning, shoelace tying) at the out-patient Institute for the Crippled and Disabled of which Gurewitsch was the Director. I felt conspicuous there, among the people of the building's name, in the building meant for me, even more conspicuous there than elsewhere.

In September, only one school year late (I could have been delayed forever), I started at General Studies, I and my mother. Two mornings a week, I would pound up the stairs of our house to the second floor, the prestige floor, grasping the banister with one hand, with my left arm around my mother's shoulder, for the balancing I needed, taking two steps per stair. Once in the upper hall, I would lean against a wall while my mother and the quietly zealous housekeeper hauled the wheelchair up to me. I was wheeled through the living room and, in the chair, backed down a small number of outdoor steps to the car, which my mother had driven up from the garage, at a level much steppier below the other side of the house. Pushing up with arms and legs, I stood and swung myself into the car. My mother and the housekeeper folded the chair and tipped, then pushed, it into the back of the car.

Down the Saw Mill River Parkway, down the Henry Hudson Parkway. We pulled up at a ramp-entrance to the campus. My mother dragged the chair from the back of the car. I hoisted myself up, hanging on to the top of the car door, and dropped into the chair. The ramp was quite steep. I hailed a student. He pushed me up the ramp. My mother pushed me along the campus walk to the classroom building. My head was self-conscious. I'd tend to keep it lowered, and sneak looks at the campus and students. I was being wheeled to college by my mother.

I, not my mother, had to be the one to ask for help—up the ramp, up stairs into the lobby of the classroom building, where I got the elevator, or else I would hiss irritation at her. Once indoors on a flat surface, I, not she, did the wheeling. If I had momentary difficulty getting out of the car, and she offered help, I would sharply warn her off. The air was made of eyes. Anything my mother did, or started to do, that I could do exposed me the more undeniably. Everything she had difficulty doing, such as getting the chair into and out of the car, made me feel more burdensome to her.

While I was in classes, my mother read a book somewhere. I did not want her in the room with me. I took American literature, Restoration drama, and two writing courses during the year. In my American literature course was a girl who didn't want to be friendly. At the end of my semester in his writing course, Padraic Colum, an Irish poet who is mentioned in Joyce's *Ulysses*, told me in a letter that my two stories "were the best, in the sense of being the most professional [I] had from the students. You have the sensitivity and the sense of language that make a writer." Joyce speaking through Colum to me.

On the way home from classes, my mother and I stopped at a service station in our neighborhood to pick up a fellow who worked there. When we got to the house, he would pull me in the chair backward up the outdoor steps and, inside, let me down the stairs in the chair. The stairs were steep, the turns were narrow. The process sounded to me like a huge piece of furniture being moved.

Whatever unnecessary helping hands I could get off my back, I felt bound to remove. If I could accustom myself to walking downstairs as well as up, I would reduce our—my—dependency on the outside helper. It was roughly twice as difficult to walk downstairs as upstairs. Because of my back's wobbling weakness, my panicky balance, I needed to walk down backward. I would not then feel about to pitch horizontally into the air. (My attitude toward gravity had become that of a slave.) The backward descent, though, went very slowly; my feet felt blind. But it meant walking instead of being carried, choice instead of enforced passivity. This was why I had learned to "walk." It took much more of more people's time, and all my strength, but it had to be done if it could be. As in going up, I used the banister and my mother's shoulder or, sometimes, my sister's. The helper followed with the empty wheelchair. Sometimes my foot would adhere to a stair; I would be unable to lift it or even kick it off and down. It infuriated me to have to ask my mother to ease the foot off the stair with her foot. The touch of her foot infuriated me. Subduing the importance of the outside helper, I added to my mother's importance. If I were walking down with my sister or the housekeeper and my mother were standing behind me as protection in case I slipped, and she took it upon herself to move a stuck foot, or a foot she thought was stuck, I snapped at her for having done it; or I would snap at her for suggesting she do it, and then, usually, have to tell her to do it; usually, when she thought I needed help, I did.

My mother got me through the school year looking professionally sober, almost gaunt with duty—ready for anything she had to take and ready not to show anything in response. She kept an absolutely even temper, as far as I know. Today, she doesn't recall my touchiness, my incessant firing of anger at the smooth surface of her devotion. I think of the year as exhausting rehearsal. She remembers her relief at what I could do, against her expectation of the year before that I would never do anything again. She was a fanatic mother.

For my part, the letter from Padraic Colum gave immediate purpose to all the stomping of my body and clanking of my wheelchair up and down the stairs; all the effort of others in my service, effort I had to accept without a counterbalancing sense of worthiness; all my embarrassment at being in the world again unconcealably different. The letter told me that, while stuck on the bank of my evolution, I had been changing. The letter said I was no longer the old kind of imitator.

FIVE

IN MY EARLIER LIFE I did not anticipate living with nouns like paralysis, rehabilitation, wheelchair; or Columbia. Even if my high school class had not been exceptionally powerful, I could not have gotten into Columbia from Fieldston with my frail grasp of scientific and mathematical concepts.

Going to Columbia, at first, unlike anything else I have done for myself in my new life, required courage. Having gotten into Columbia, I would have to manage *being* there. I didn't know whether I could do it, what it would ask of me. I just went; dove. I had to move "out," to catch up with my own life. My high school friends would have graduated from college three months before I was to start my official junior year. I had to get out of the dining room of my parents' house, away from women who had to drive me everywhere I went, who dumped my shit for me, who sat behind me when I wanted privacy, who could tell me when a guest of mine should leave. I wanted to learn to live by my wits, to learn what wits I had. I was going to have to depend imaginatively on others and myself: that's what took the courage. How would I get from dorm to class? Who would dump my shit for me now? Not women, but who? I still needed the aid of an enema. What looked like, and was, freedom to me—the choosing of courses at a school I was proud to be attending, the choosing of new friends, the chance to learn what my sexual future would be, the chance to learn a new New

York, to move in a society as a full-time person—meant *taking* chances, meant personal and physical hitchhiking, meant learning, now that I had survived myself, how to survive.

Even more than my surviving implied the need, still, to rely on others, to impose my weakness on the strength of others, to be "carried," it implied relying on others as little as I could. Self-dependence, no matter how arduous, had to be easier for me than taking help. There were two ways for me to get from my dormitory to Hamilton Hall, where classes were held. One way meant asking a student to wheel me across the quadrangle, then, at the foot of Hamilton, asking additional students for help up the considerable number of steps. I did this for a few days, but it meant not only asking for help, it meant waiting for someone cheerful, though not too cheerful, going in the right direction, to ask. I learned that under the quadrangle, connecting the dorms and Hamilton Hall, ran a tunnel, and I arranged to use it (one needed permission), taking the dorm elevator down, and pushing myself the block's distance in the indoor twilight, past the steam-pipes and areas of stored equipment. At the far end was a rise too steep for me to push myself up. Here I had to wait, often as long as twenty minutes, for a janitor to come along to assist me. But waiting for help in the tunnel did not seem to cost me as much as waiting in public. The less I needed from fewer people, and the less conspicuously, the safer I felt. The more I relied on myself, the less chance I imagined I had of getting stuck, on the principle that the simpler one's life is, the less chance it has of breaking down. Asking a janitor's help, I was already, on my own power, almost where I needed to be. (And, I felt, a janitor, more than a fellow-student, was accustomed to pushing, wheeling.)

Finally, into the basement of Hamilton Hall, and the elevator. I was never late for classes; their excellence itself had to be studied: the devout intensiveness of Hieatt's Chaucer course; Shenton's exuberant, myth-scorning American history; modern poetry, taught by Dupee, so intimate with his amazing amount of information that he delivered it as if it were anecdote; Andrew Chiappe's magnificent year-long Shakespeare, the lectures dramatic, their revelations unearthed by Chiappe from way beneath where we could see to, awesome finds of originality; the luxurious writing tutorial, in which the stories, poems, or novels-in-progress of the students chosen for the course were criticized by the professor at a weekly private session. The dull gray corridor through which I laboriously wheel-stroked let out in a house of stages where masters of interpretation performed. These men were the equal of my father in authority and accomplishment, and I understood their language, as he would not have. I moved sideways to move upward.

Back at the home end of the tunnel, beyond my dorm's elevator, I could take another elevator into another dormitory, John Jay Hall, on one floor of which were offices of campus organizations, including the newspaper, the literary magazine, and the humor magazine, *Jester*. I began to visit the cordial *Jester* office after morning classes, and it was soon the humor magazine, and not the literary magazine, that I joined. The members of the literary magazine were not enemies of the campus at Columbia, as they'd been at Middlebury, but, even if they had been, I wouldn't have joined them; they seemed to me to walk close to the wall. They reminded me just enough of my fringe state at Middlebury, where I'd *had* to join the literary magazine.

Jester had never been a jock or a yock magazine. In fact, it could be criticized for being too subdued, gentlemanly, as if it wished it were *The New Yorker*. But I could overlook a little imitation elegance; it seemed harmless, and it was tempting. And *Jester*, at the core, was original, especially in the cartoons of the toothy but unterrifying monsters, and of the terrifying, manically imbecile women, and of the men grinning with inappropriate pride, by Edward Koren. I revered the charming hatred in Koren's drawings of people. They had made him (now a beloved *New Yorker* cartoonist) a campus idol. I wanted to be, as he was, central; and I wanted to make fun of while making fun, to kick at while kicking up. By the time I had settled well in at Columbia, I was eager to engage cordially—meaning above all humorously—with the life around me, to win laughter and to laugh, as I had not been able to do since Fieldston. The unearned, puritanical contempt I'd shown at Middlebury for my immediate human surroundings had vanished. The immediate human surroundings had improved, too. But I discovered that, post-accident, my anger, like an internal organ, had enlarged. My emotional blood was no longer solemn, but alertly irritable. I could not ignore anything that imagined itself to be other than what it was —as I had imagined myself to be at Middlebury—or anything that tried to mislead, or to conceal itself. I had sharp eyes and ears for the woman (head tipped at the slant people use for appreciating babies) smiling at me on the street; for soulfulness, jargon, gushiness, glibness, lip-service, scene-stealing, personal melodrama. The fake was repulsive to me because of its *danger*. Self-awareness, for everyone, meant safety.

I reconciled my regained cheerfulness and my newly developed anger by trying to make funny what I found dangerous. The mimicking I had performed physically in high school turned literary. The pages of *Jester* allowed, as they cooled, my private fear and my disgusts. My need to warn came out as parodies, usually of institutions beyond the campus: pompous magazines, self-serving letters to the editor, commerical come-ons, highfalutin record-liner notes. The parodies, with a few exceptions over two years, had little chance of offending their subjects, but they relieved me.

I learned forever at Columbia that the people I was likely to love the most were instinctive satirists or responsive to satirists. The sense, or appreciation, of satire I took from then on to mean accurate vision, honesty, trustworthiness. I came to know that the people I trusted took parts of me (much the same parts we each took of ourselves) to mock—my paranoia, my anxiety, my dogmatism (a satirist is convinced), my blunt fondness for attention, and comic aspects of my odd physical situation. The people

I trusted loved me enough, understood me enough, to give me my true place, to spare me exemption from the rules of common reality. And they laughed when I meant to be funny, too.

My other social focal point was the famous West End Bar, at 113th Street and Broadway. Late at night, a friend and I would often go there for beer and a sandwich, and the swarm. An uptown bohemia gathered at the West End, students from Columbia and Barnard, ex-students, pre-artists, artists, and ex-artists. Among the regulars was a dancer named Joanne, whom I came to know. She eventually introduced me to a younger friend of hers, Nicole. Nicole was no satirist. But it seemed more important at the time that she was no Margaret. Nicole gleamed with joy and full-fledged, long-haired beauty. She strode; she smiled a lot, and ardently. She was all *open*. Her openness and beauty, her sweetness, her cheerfulness, and her reciprocity were all any man could want.

Nicole began coming to see me at Columbia in the evenings. Women were not yet allowed upstairs in the men's dorms, so she would wheel me out onto the campus in the cold dark. She would sit on a bench, and I in my chair, and we would reach to embrace and kiss. We became, of course, impatient with embracing and kissing in the cold, as if across a small table. But we had no convenient place to lie down in. One night I took her to a concert on campus. She made herself an innocently dramatic dress of much blue chiffon, a costume more than a dress, a gown for a dance number. Joanne arranged to leave her nearby apartment free for us. After the performance, Koren wheeled me to Joanne's apartment, Nicole walking beside me. I was not ready to let her tip me up and down curbs. Koren and Nicole walking, I being wheeled. We could have been going anywhere, the three of us together, probably Koren and Nicole belonging to each other, I a friend. In fact, it was Koren delivering me to bed with Nicole. No one on the street would have imagined that.

Koren left us. In the tiny apartment, we undressed on the bed.

For me, the moment meant a reunion with desire itself. I was hungry. It had been a year and a half since I'd seen a naked female body. It had been two and a half years since I'd wanted to see a naked female body. It had been three and a half years since I'd seen a new naked female body. Here was a new, beautiful, and loving one. What was I to do with it? The excitement in my head was not reaching my penis. I buried my face in Nicole's crotch and busied myself there.

Nicole lacked nothing but those qualities of brain—information, "seriousness," analytical intensity, verbal confidence, satirical alertness—that I needed to value but had not yet known in a woman able, through age or inherent good fortune, to be physically open as well, like Nicole. I adored her available virtues, until I grew impatient with the charming simplicity, the pure sweetness, the general gusto, the radiant beauty. As I showed my impatience, she clung cheerfully—proof to me that her brain didn't lie behind her eyes but was divided among her muscles. I snapped us apart one afternoon a few weeks after we had joined, out of tact and confusion presenting a set of general excuses. I couldn't be sure that the reason I needed so decisively to sever myself from Nicole wasn't the failure of my penis to love her very openness, wasn't a terror of being received. To her, I was evidently nothing like a failure. She did not want to lose me. Two years later, lonely for all her qualities that had so quickly bored me, I tried to retrieve her, but she had disappeared from the phone book.

In the brief experience following the relatively exalted weeks with Nicole, I had as my partner a self-styled hot little piece from Barnard who kissed me tongue-ily in public and talked a great deal about our making what she called "mad, passionate love," and who, when we finally lay naked in bed on a weekend visit to my parents', burst into tears as I lodged my hand in her groin, and fled upstairs to her room. Had I known then, as I later learned, that Vaso did a lot of nude prancing around her dorm, that she enjoyed gynecological examinations, that she was occasionally a stern devotee of her stern church, while at other times she shouted, crazily *meaning* it, her right to extravagant hedonistic privileges—"I should be lying on a silk couch while men feed me grapes!"—I would have gone out with her anyway. At the time, I must have wanted experience as such, as much as I wanted whatever intimacy is.

Then I met Lizzie. Lizzie, also a Barnard student (otherwise of a different species, a different genus, from Vaso's), interrupted "experience." Lizzie had a reliably impressive intelligence—she defined thoughts, themes, personalities, as superior intelligence does, in a simultaneously lucid and imaginative fashion—and she had a vivid emotional range, strong in both cheerfulness and tenderness. She was above all a satirist, an intellectual comedienne, a joke-teller of spontaneous events, a lover of human surprises. A chance remark of peculiar stupidity would make her day. She could be belligerently vulnerable, but her exceptional alertness to the weak points in others, and her skill in improvised parody, and her unusual amount of vitality kept her safe most of the time. She could make possible, I must have felt, the merging of my lust for the hard-brained woman with my lust for the woman happily eager in her sexual desire; the merging of my left-over sense of "maturity," "responsibility," with a guiltless, fearless acquiescence in the sharp tugging of the body I had been born with twice.

In over twenty months of intimacy, Lizzie and I never tried for sexual completion. We never tried to try. We cooperated in sexual restraint from start to finish. The intensifying of our closeness carried with it the intensifying of our caution. We sprayed caution at one another as if it were disinfectant. We would lie on the bed of a friend in the city, or occasionally on my bed at home, our clothes off, and play with each other, and be content. Or we would lock the door of the *Jester* office and fiddle like experimenting children, with the utmost intimacy but as if we didn't know there was more. I was then nearly twenty-three.

We were free talking in dorm lobbies, going to the theater, restaurants. We moved quite a bit around the city together, I by this time accustomed to using taxicabs. Our enthusiasm for one another's clothed company, skulled brains, was luxuriously comfortable, encouraging, *gay*. We had the lovers' sense of infinite interest in each other and in ourselves together, and the lovers' ability to invigorate actual interestingness. Even though slackened nerves, or fear of connecting, or of failing to connect, continued more or less to keep me sexually shrunken, I loved to excite Lizzie; and even though she had inhibitions of her own, her response to my hands showed the happy eagerness I'd hoped for. Yet my merging of intellectual and sexual need took place largely above her neck.

Unknown to me for a time—(a problem I hadn't raised myself)—within Lizzie's skull lived parents who would be nervous, if not humiliated, to learn that their nineteen-year-old daughter was in love with a would-be writer in a wheelchair; that she spent as much time as she could with someone whose love for her could deny her a predictable, adequate future in which they could take pride. Lizzie had always set out not to upset her parents. I would upset them. It would not serve that I was evidently talented and healthy, or that I made Lizzie feel valuable and distinctive. Distinction was beside their point. It would be important to them, rather, that since life was already difficult—this they acknowledged—one shouldn't go asking for more trouble. I was more trouble.

Not long after Lizzie had indicated to her mother that we were close in a way that suggested "trouble" (though marriage had not become an issue for us), she told me, in fear of telling me, that her parents seriously disapproved of such a friendship with such a man. I heard Lizzie calmly. I told her, she remembers, that it was "sensible" of her to tell me; and I "understood" how hard it was for her to tell me. Lizzie didn't want to quit, though. In fact, as she sees it today, to have told me and not to want to quit deepened her claim on me. She was confirming her love by going against disapproval. But her message from her mother amounted to a first step in a long sequence of unconscious negotiations for our disentanglement.

When my calmness had settled down, rage took over. The calmness, really, was the first phase of the rage: it recognized the possibility that Lizzie's mother was right to warn her daughter against me. The rules of common reality, which I so wanted to be required to obey, as an immigrant to a new existence, had abruptly toughened. It wasn't my fault, I had been informed, but I was bad.

The problem boiled up. I had the sense, again, of others' weakness being stronger than my strength. How widespread would the weakness turn out to be? Fear could run. I could not chase after to explain that I was not fearsome. Fear did not have to listen, would not listen. I had become a person to avoid. I had never been a person to avoid. In my earlier life I had been much loved. In my new life, I'd had the additional advantage, so far, of being esteemed. But now I learned that someone could feel I was soiled. Someone could be everyone. I had been told: "Leave our daughter alone. You will damage her life. Be generous. Deprive yourself." I had, suddenly, a record, a tainted history. I was black, or an alcoholic, or crippled, something like that. *I* wasn't crippled. I had never been crippled before, never been black. Was something wrong with Lizzie that she loved me?

What was I doing here? Should I, just when I was learning my strength, teach myself not to respond to women because I couldn't otherwise help causing them trouble, or at the least leading them into dead ends? I could not believe it. I had pulled myself up a sheer cliffside of the earth, in the dark, hanging over nothing but space, and attained level ground. It made no sense that I shouldn't enjoy my amazing salvation, it made no sense that I shouldn't act victorious. Was I being told to *pretend* to live, that I would be paid in admiration for keeping clear of actual engagement, while showing a cheerful spirit that people like Lizzie's mother could applaud with relief? Was I supposed to be plucky, in other words, but not too plucky? Was I supposed not to ask and give, not to make mistakes, not to create my share of problems? Was my share automatically too much? Were the rules different for me? Who was to make them? And what were they to be?

In the meantime, Lizzie and I acted according to our devotion. If her parents were right, it was only because the way they put it —that one shouldn't go *asking* for trouble—they couldn't be wrong, only incomplete. Certain kinds of asked-for trouble have to be preferable to many kinds of trouble that can't be anticipated (no matter how much one prefers predictability), as twenty years of richly varied domestic and physical disasters all about me show.

During summer vacation, in 1956, I went to stay with my brother and sister-in-law and their baby son in their house on an ordnance depot in Sidney, Nebraska—an unspoiled vacation spot revealed by my new life—where my brother was fulfilling his military obligation as the depot's doctor. On the flight, I wore a rubber apparatus meant to make one free to urinate in public secretly. The thing fitted over my penis like a heavy condom. A tube ran from the condom to a rubber bag strapped to my calf. The device was intolerable to me, like the electric hand, or like a back-brace Gurewitsch had suggested that, to my mother's fury, I rigidly refused to wear. (Gurewitsch was able to assure her that my refusal could safely take precedence over the brace.) For urinating, I had been using a small enamel chamber pot wrapped, when I was out of the house, in a paisley silk muffler and tucked under my jacket. At college, when necessary, I would wheel myself from the classroom into the men's room, use the pot, pour the contents into the standing urinal, rinse it out, wrap it up, tuck it under my jacket again, and return to class. At the theater with Lizzie, I was able to use it comfortably, under my coat, in the dark, directing or timing my stream for maximum silence, without attracting any attention. But on the plane I would be in the open. So I tried the rubber apparatus.

By the time I reached Denver, where my brother and his wife met me with their car, the lap of my pants was soaked. Some of my urine had run backward, according to my obtuse slant in the airplane seat. By using my portable urinal, under a jacket or an airplane blanket, I would have been able to arrange myself, to see what I was doing; it would have been necessary. Explaining myself to, or concealing my act from, a seatmate could not be as distressing as it was to have wet my pants in public.

Occasionally at night, people think: I am going to die some-day; my life will be over forever; my brain, my memory, my future, will be someone else's air; I will never be back. Over the summer at the ordnance depot, which for me was a place out-side reality, I thought about my future on the other side of the country with a similarly appalled sense of permanent conclusion. Only my panic meant there might be alternatives; at least I was asking myself what the alternatives could possibly be. I would return East, to my remaining year of college, but then what? I had one year left in my wallet. Where would I get the rest of my life from? I'd moved out of paralysis, out of bed, out of my par-ents' house, into college, into the city, among people. After col-lege, would I have to go back into my parents' house? I had no wish for graduate school. I felt delayed already; I wanted to live among all the choices there were, among the difficulties I had earned. That was why I had worked my way out of my par-ents' house. But how would I manage farther out? And doing what? Where would I live among the choices? How much more flexibility would I need? Had I already reached my limit? Would I always need somebody with me? Urinating on a plane was, for me, like having no floor beneath me, no net to my life. I could fall for miles. I was exposed.

The plane trip seemed to have shown me what I had heard Lizzie's mother say—that I should stay away from full participa-tion. Never since the accident had it occurred to me that I might not be meant to *be*. Now it appeared possible my future had been laid out in such a way that my salvation would be brief, a passing experience, like being in the hospital. Even though I'd earned it, I might not be able to keep it. This injustice made perfect sense, not because I felt bitter or felt I was meant to be gypped. It made perfect sense because I had learned, at the point of the accident, that there was no inevitable injustice or justice, that nothing necessarily followed anything sensibly or proportionately, that anything could happen to anyone at any time. If I had "asked" for my accident, or if my accident was the "right" accident for me, that did not mean it wasn't an accident. I had not wished a broken neck on myself. I had not been thinking ahead. I had merely been miserable and angry. I could have been miserable and angry for the rest of my life and not broken my neck.

I knew it was possible that the nighttime kinds of thoughts I stared at in Nebraska might signify nothing about the future except that its invisibility terrified me. Columbia had been unknown the year before, and I had learned it (even found students in the next room willing to dump my bedpan). Still, Columbia could happen to have been easy—and life beyond it turn out to be impossibly difficult—for my muscles. I trusted the reach of my will, but I had to be uncertain about the extent of my literal reach, and I had to wonder what I would be allowed to touch.

Jester remained a safe, sunny place for me. I gained strength there. At the end of the previous year, Koren had been elected Editor-in-Chief and I Managing Editor. Now, as seniors, we had a magazine. We made the policy, we wrote the editorials, and we did most of the centerspreads, drawings by him, text by me. We were well received. To our unique advantage was the College's proposal, that year, of a compulsory Citizenship program—activity on the part of the students, for academic credit, in local Morningside Heights, a largely black slum neighborhood. Tutoring, painting of apartments, guitar- and ping-pong-playing: we were supposed to keep the neighborhood company and improve its well-being. Koren and I had a high-point in our centerspread pointing up the comical impracticality of the idea. But our chief motive in objecting to the proposal was not, in fact, its impracticality, as we judged it, or any condescension or missionary imperialism suggested by the students' role. It was, rather—at the beginning of the late fifties—that students should not be asked to behave as a public group. We thought college was the last time we would have the chance to be as private, as self-centered, as we wished to be (I thought this even as I feared becoming, after college, far more private than I wished to be). We thought, even more basically, that no one should be asked to be the same as everyone else. And we thought that no one should be asked to be "good" in a single way determined by a single authority other than ourselves. The proposal reminded me forcefully of Ethical Culture and its expectation of selflessness. It threatened the part of me that got significant pleasure from choosing to be different, and it threatened the part of me that got pleasure from being nasty at a distance. My civic duty, in effect, was to satirize civic duty. Others should do what they wanted to do; but only what they wanted to do.

When our anti-Citizenship issue had been published, Lionel Trilling, a preeminent professor of English, saw me across the campus and walked a long way out of his way to congratulate me on *Jester*'s mockery of the Citizenship program. Applause from such approved authority would have been enough response for me, but we got more; we got results. The Citizenship program was not instituted. We felt we had made a difference.

If my father were to complain, as I fantasized he might, that our attitude had been superior, mischievous, pointlessly provocative, I would have the professor's congratulations to prove me responsible. Trilling was not only world-famous, he was famous for his careful considerations of moral issues. I wanted it both ways—to be nasty, at a distance, and to be excused by the angered object, actual or symbolic, for my nastiness. From a very narrow strip, I had for years been able to tease my father, to our mutual pleasure. His portliness was one safe subject; the other was his wandering singing voice. If I stepped off the strip, I stepped on his toes, risked punishment. Punishment was, in fact, no more than a spasm of his irritability, but in my mind that spasm was a dangerous electric current, it could do me physical harm. Or I feared the expansion of his irritability into one of his rages; but his rages were vocal too, no more physical than a stomping in the hall and the slamming of a door. I seem to have felt that the man who had never laid an angry hand on me could kill me with his voice; or that one day his voice would enter his hands. I had generalized my teasing of him into nastiness at a distance; but there was no being away from him; there was no distance. No matter what I happened to be mocking, I feared and I daydreamed his angry response. Everything provocative that I did, I did for him: I wished for his punishment while I wished for his laughter.

On the occasional weekends that I went home, Koren sometimes came to visit so that we could do *Jester* work. Once, when we were reviewing material for a forthcoming issue, my father trotted down to the dining room to say hello. We showed him a piece, by a staff member, that delighted us, a nonsense version of a political ad. It went on, for a full page, in this manner: "Slattle Poronyl/ Forinnal Colottiny/ Pennegal Crottinox/ *Et forgootle plootben ognitz Eisenhower?*/ NYEXBRTVOG-GEN!!/CORIVINNITZ NIXON!!"

My father's response started with a sneeze of a laugh and gave up to runaway squealing. Each time he seemed to have stopped, he took off again, sobbing laughter, the piece of paper in his hands irresistible to his wet eyes. It took a number of minutes, during which Koren and I got to laughing at my father's laughter as hard as he was laughing, for him and for us to subside. My father was no Eisenhower man, but Eisenhower was President; in any case, politics was serious. I saw my father laughing ecstatically, an ally of "my" magazine, overjoyed at our disrespect. I saw my president laughing at his President. I was able to be fairer to my father after this; I did not need to love fearing him so. I had finally lived long enough to see him acting like me.

Not that we were finished being father and son; but we started to relax our responses to one another. I began to see as manageable what had once been tyrannical. I began to see that a dictate of his needn't mean an abashed, obedient answer or an obliquely rebellious answer on my part. I could, I saw, giving myself room and time to think and breathe, be diplomatic on my own behalf. I had written a long satirical poem, to be published in *Jester* (and a few years later to be my first commercial publication, in *Saturday Review*), about the tendency of literary works to go through as many changes of form as the market could be made to bear—a story, a play, a movie, a stage musical, a movie musical, and more. I had never achieved such sustained smoothness, shown such assurance, in anything I'd done before. I handed the poem to my parents when they were visiting me one evening. My father, physician, safety expert, but not poet, noticed that one of the lines had a little extra foot in it. I said yes, I knew that, it belonged there. He said it spoiled the poem, none of the other lines had an extra foot. To myself I wondered whether he could possibly be right; was the extra foot an awkward bump, or was it helpful to the line, as I had once known it to be? No one else had said anything about it, I said, growing warm as I contained my anger. My father continued to fuss, as if I had done something careless, risky. It had come down to my words now, when I was almost twenty-four, his anxiety that I watch what I was doing. A bump in a line of poetry was something one could trip over. He knew a famous poet. Would I send her, or let him send her, my poem for examination? More contraceptive advice. I did not say, as I should have, no, this is not your field, and I know what I am doing. But I did not, either, say yes. I temporized. It would be uncomfortable, I said, to send the poem to her, but I would think about it. And the matter died. *Jester* did me nothing but good.

It appeared that writing might be going to give me biological flexibility. My *Jester* pieces were popular, most of my academic papers were getting high marks, and the stories I was working on in the writing tutorial were attracting encouragement. A story I submitted to the literary magazine's annual contest won first prize and was duly published. But I could not, and did not want to, rely on my writing for a livelihood. I wanted a job, if there was one for me that would satisfy me, among people. Andrew Chiappe, my Shakespeare professor and one of my writing tutors, was associated as a consultant with the publishing firm of Doubleday and Company. He suggested I apply there to become an editorial trainee. He and several other professors wrote me recommendations. So, in midwinter of my senior year, I had arrived at the turn in my life that I had anticipated, without being able to see, from Nebraska the summer before. I was about to find out what my life would be like. The kind of next day we know is going to be critical, without knowing in which of two or three possible directions, had come.

Accompanied by my friend Stan Lubman, I went downtown one afternoon to the Doubleday offices. I saw the Personnel Director, a dramatically obese woman. All her obesity had been converted to kindliness, and all her kindliness was reaching for me. Under the circumstances, I managed not to seem to notice. It looked as if it had been decided beforehand that I was to be hired. I told her I would have to find an apartment convenient for me; she said Doubleday would try to help. I told her I would need a roommate, for safety's sake and to split the rent with. (The trainee salary started at sixty-five dollars a week.) Doubleday should be able to help, she said; one of the other trainees would likely be looking for a roommate, too. I wafted upstairs to talk with the Managing Editor and others. They explained to me in detail what a trainee did. They looked forward to my joining them after my graduation.

Well, I looked forward to joining them. Lubman and I took a cab up to the West End, where we met Lizzie. I got drunk. I would not be surprised if I talked about the social worker at the Rusk Institute who had recommended I be trained for lens-grinding. When we left the bar, we were all laughing at anything. Lubman was having trouble pushing the wheelchair over the heavily snow-covered cobbles of ice on the sidewalk. Eventually, jolted by a bump and relaxed by relief and Scotch, I capsized from the chair. I lay on my back in the snow, screaming laughter as if I were watching a beautiful surprise in a slapstick movie. Lubman and Lizzie were laughing nearly as hard. Lubman and some astonished passers-by got me back into the chair.

Lizzie and I had been continuing to spend time together as intimately and energetically as before, but with interruptions, now, for seeing others. Lizzie was in love with me but couldn't, quite, love me; I was not finding, in my less than half-hearted wandering, anyone else to love.

Our atmosphere was so ambiguous that we were sometimes together when we were out with others. Lizzie's mother's arm was set between us; neither of us could knock it aside. The arm was like a curse. It made us make fools of ourselves, so that we would offend each other. On the New Year's Eve that led into 1957, Lizzie and I, separately, went to a party at Lubman's girlfriend's house, in Brooklyn. I was "with" Louise, a classmate of Lizzie's. I urged Louise to join me upstairs in a bedroom. Our meeting could not be discreet. I had to get up there. With help, in full view of the party, I stomped slowly up the stairs, someone dragging the wheelchair after. Louise and I lay down on a bed. I hardly knew her, but she was attractive and interested. Also, she told me now, she was having her period. We soon got up, exchanging apologies. Louise went downstairs and sent help to get me down.

In the spring, Lizzie threw a public fit of possessiveness that frightened me, as it was meant to, and entrapped a particularly shy, decent friend of ours as mediator. The arm tortured us. But we kept trying to outwit it.

She gave me a copy of Wallace Stevens's "Harmonium" for my graduation: "June 4, 1957/ To R. P. Brickner, B.A./ Much love, Lizzie." The day was so sunny, I had trouble seeing. In the glare, I could best make out my parents. We had gotten here. We hadn't expected to be here in this dazzling collision of past, present, and future at all.

SIX

TO BE HIRED was to be invited further into the world. But I was the one who had to get there and figure out how to live there. I was not my own host. My host's implied confidence in my adaptability did not prove my adaptability. On the day I was hired (and I poured out of my wheelchair into the snow), I had felt that my future was taken care of, when, in fact, it had been no more than declared a possibility.

It was to my parents' house that I returned after Columbia. It was my mother, again, who drove me downtown. I worked at Doubleday—at first writing (on an electric typewriter) "flap copy," the explanatory praise that goes into book jackets—two or three days a week. I slept over at the apartments of friends or their parents. I was able to spend two or three nights away from my home base because I moved my bowels (still with an enema but on the toilet now) once every three or four days. The procedure, though, was too lengthy and complicated to use in anyone else's house. My mother picked me up at the Doubleday office at the end of my rich man's week.

But not much more than a month passed before an apartment I could live in had been located, looked over, and rented. A long, skinny hall painted a creamed orange color that disturbed the stomach, a tiny bathroom, a kitchenette, a living room (where my roommate would sleep) the same color as the hall, its one window looking out on a wall two inches away, and a bedroom whose windows looked out on a plot of weeds and garbage and didn't quite close. The apartment was on the ground floor—no getting stuck in the uncertain elevator—and the entrance to the building had only one step. I would need to be tipped up it and let down it, but since two steps would have made the building impracticable for me, one step could seem like none. The rent for the ugly and hideously furnished but convenient apartment was just manageable by me and Cal, a polite, ordinary-seeming fellow from the South, who had been living at the YMCA. Cal looked to me like a freshman seminarian, small, smooth, clean; like a Christian before anything else. The personnel woman at Doubleday, in seeking a roommate for me out of the trainees, had seen him the same way, I supposed.

In midsummer of 1957, Cal and I moved into the apartment on First Avenue and 65th Street, deep in the city, everything taller to me by a few feet than it would normally be, and seeming far taller than that. To see the city as too big for me altogether, as I couldn't help doing at moments—too tall, thick, wide, long—made it seem amazing to me that I was able to move around in it. Taxi wheels and engines, elevators: I incorporated the principles that aided me into myself. I could speed, like everybody. I was amazing to me. I was nearest to being on my own at just the point in my evolution where the demands on my adjustability were the most various; and I was able, at a time in history of mechanical sophistication necessary to my "independence" (at a time in history that had been able to keep me alive), and in a city that typified this sophistication, almost completely to absorb these demands. The city that made it hard made it easy.

My practical life took on the shape suggested by Thomas Hardy's remark to the effect that the writer's job is to make the great small and the small great. My major problems were minor, but the minor ones stuck out. Nothing was more important for me to recognize, on a street or on a written page, than the possibilities of the minor. A crack or bump could spill the wheelchair, if it was going fast enough, just as a misplaced comma or an ambiguous word can spill a sentence. I had told Cal that he was not responsible for me, that his schedule must in no way depend on mine, that there was nothing out of the way he'd have to do for me. So sometimes we would leave for Doubleday together and sometimes we would not. On the days we left separately, or in the evenings when I was going out alone and Cal wasn't around, I would have to wait for someone coming through the lobby to let me down the front step. On weekday mornings, I did not usually have long to wait. Occasionally, though, a lot of slow minutes could pass, while I sat like a doorman with nothing to do, energy without available activity, self-wasting. (Once, while waiting for help, I made an idiot's face through the glass door leading to the street, enacting for myself what a facially distorted helpless person would look like to a passer-by. A passer-by happened to look my way before I could retrieve my own expression.) I would not hail people from outside the door for help down the step, not wanting to startle them—more than that, not wanting to attract any more attention to my dependency than I could avoid doing. A fellow-tenant, even if a stranger, lived on my side of the line. A stranger off the street would have to see me as more of an intrusion, I felt.

The more someone was a stranger to me, or the more someone was a woman my age, the more I wanted to keep the wheelchair I sat in a secret. But all I turned out to need by way of cooperation from others in my wish to keep my conspicuousness secret was a straightforward, if not indifferent, attitude. The direct, the casually realistic, view of me ignored me by making the least of me as a physical problem. But often people known to the general public as "well-meaning" came at me, smiling the threat of their interest. "On my own" in the city, I was twenty-four, in a wheelchair, sitting among walkers. Elevators, taxis, enhanced me, but elevator operators and taxi drivers could humiliate me. If I was tired or nervous, the wrong friendly word or the wrong friendly pat on the shoulder made me feel like a twenty-four-year-old in a perambulator. When I asserted my dependency, I remained my own boss. Asked to be, or told I was, dependent, I could feel instantly exposed, as if my secret was out, as I had felt misurinating on the plane to Nebraska. Strangers, especially, were dangerous to me. Offering me unnecessary help or paying me unnecessary attention, they were saying to me, "Boy, look at you. Did *you* fuck up. You need help. I'll help you." They were deciding for me. If a theater usher asked the person I was with, "Can he get out of his chair?" I was such a mistake I couldn't even be addressed. Embarrassed to fury, I would not express the fury for fear of making a scene outside myself, embarrassing others with the heat of my embarrassment. If I sat at a street corner, waiting to catch a cab, and someone approached me to ask, "Do you want to cross the street?" I felt I was being told I did not—because I could not—know what I was doing. "No, thank you, I'm waiting to get a cab." "Do you want me to help you get a cab?" "No, thanks, I'll take care of it." "Are you sure?" "I'll take care of it, I said." Worse was to notice a stranger, especially a woman two generations older than I (the most common category), hailing a cab for me, pointing me out to a cab. My lungs would smoke, and I would choke on the smoke, or I would yell, embarrassed *beyond* embarrassment, "Stay out of it!" "I'm sorry," the woman would say, "I was only trying to help." And she was, and she wasn't. Or: I would hail a cab, and it would pull up cozily. And the driver would step out and come around to me and say, in a calm, friendly voice, "Tell me what I can do." And I would say, in a calm, friendly voice, "If you'll just hold the door stiff, please, I'll get myself in. The chair folds up and can go in the front or in the trunk." I would push down, stand up, grab the door, step, start to swivel. Hands gripping my arm, pushing at my back. A woman in white saying, "I'm a nurse, I know what to do." I (after I'd shouted "Jesus, let go!"): "But I'm not a patient!" Clever, ineffective. The interfering nurse was "only trying to help." Or: I would hail a cab, and it would pull up cozily. The driver would step out. As he came around to me I would see that he walked with a limp so severe he appeared to be falling sideways, backward, and directly downward with every other step. His voice would carry for a block, announcing me, announcing us: "Now what can I do for you, young fellow? You just tell me! We all have to help each other out, right?" The halt leading the halt, I would give my line of instruction, but subduedly, trying to hide from his raucous comradeship. "I guess you like to do it yourself! Some people, they don't like to help themselves at all!" Degrading praise. The whole street must be watching, I would think. I'd stand, grab the door, step, swivel. "You really have that down to a science, don't you? I was in one of those wagons myself for four months!" And then I'd sit watching the driver's prolonged, sloppy struggle to get the wheelchair in. Or the waitress at the cheapest decent restaurant near Doubleday, who would urge me to join a wheelchair baseball team on Long Island she knew about. I could not tell her how much I didn't want to join a wheelchair baseball team often enough or in enough different ways. On days I managed to avoid sitting in her section, she'd make her way to me and exhort me. I was not able to be rude enough to stop her.

There could also be too much indifference. One freezing afternoon, I left Doubleday at rush hour. The sidewalk seemed jammed with people watching a fast parade of occupied taxis. I spotted one, unoccupied, coming along, and waved desperately. As it zipped past, I screamed "Cocksucker!" humiliating myself. At difficult taxi times, after that, I trundled around the corner to a hotel, moving under the wing of the canopy, under the wing of the huge doorman with his whistle, gratefully giving myself up to help. I wanted others to be as realistic about me as I was. An unrealistic, egocentric, necessary wish.

I did not know what was realistic for Lizzie and me. We had never thought to define our future, but as soon as Lizzie's realistic mother had defined it as troublesome, it started to disappear on us. I had no value for Lizzie's family—no career, no wealth, no expectation of the full physical normality their peace of mind demanded, no indication that I'd be able to father a child. I was only four years old in my new life. I did not know what I had—or would ever have—to offer a girlfriend's family. I knew that Lizzie and I loved and enlivened each other, and that we had been poisoned so that we—I—would be unable to poison her mother, father, uncles, and aunts. While Lizzie and I continued to spend time together secretly, now at my apartment, and to talk daily on the phone, all with the old energy, that energy marked time. It grew easy to see that one of us would quit at the first good chance we got.

The first chance I had was not good enough to quit Lizzie for, but it was good enough to predict a future for me in which I could afford to leave her. At Doubleday, as part of my job in the flap-copy department, I was working on a catalogue of forthcoming books. Working with me was an entertaining and unmistakably pretty girl named Connie. The glints of her interest in me could not be misunderstood. One day we went home to the apartment after work, and almost immediately to bed. Nothing important happened there. I remember her nakedness, so much less powerful than Lizzie's, and our mild fervor. Though we remained friendly, that was our one time in bed together. But my getting to bed, into bed, with someone new, someone else, showed me that out in the city in my new life, I was attractive, attractive to the attractive. If I had been picked once, I would be picked again; and I had been encouraged to do my own picking.

Not long after Connie's visit, I and Lizzie destroyed our formal love. In my bedroom, I told her I was done. She got panicky, her voice kept swelling. She wanted us to lie on the bed. I got onto the bed with her. We touched as if we were scrambling in lust, but the frantic strokes felt to me like hatred, ripping, punishment, her mother's arm jerking us. I wanted Lizzie to vanish, wanted never to have known her, never to know of her again. Decisive freedom would be like sexual completion. I got up, we got up, from the bed. I told her and I told her that we were no good anymore, that we must start all over again separately. I could not understand why she didn't understand. Why was she pleading? What was she pleading for? The chaos of our feelings made the air seem wrecked, as if it were filling with overturned furniture and dust. I got desperate at the endurance of Lizzie's panic. I felt locked into the room with her. I put my head to my knee and bit it. I shouted at her to go, then, and she went.

On a Friday in September, at a party, I saw a girl hurrying to the buffet table, and I sprang at her desirability, rolling myself toward her, fast. She was small, lucky in body, with a lovely, preoccupied face and long, thick hair of a hazy red. I felt her to be alone; how could she be alone? This prize and I introduced ourselves (she seemed to have hoped and known I would follow her) and then, sitting together at the other side of the room, reviewed the recent theater. Jill was only eighteen, so her impatient standards and opinions had an admirable confidence to them. She had just started college, at New York University. She responded happily to me. And she was physically so charming that I wanted to lick her forever. We talked to no one else until we were interrupted by the arrival of her boyfriend. But by then we had agreed I was to phone her the next morning.

The next morning we arranged easily that she would come to my apartment that evening. I didn't ask about Tom, the boyfriend. I went through the day with my body vibrating finely. When Jill arrived—I remember opening the door to her, finding there exactly the same adorable girl I had met the night before— we went to the bedroom. She sat in a green armchair and I to the left of her chair, our chairs parallel. We talked for fewer than five minutes before we slowly grabbed each other and kissed. I had not felt excited so deeply—my heart with one dry beat knocked the blood from my head—since the years before Margaret, when kisses could alarm the body. I remember our solemnity as we moved to the bed. I don't remember whether we tried to fuck, only that we didn't, but that it was as if we had. I remember our sense of being stricken with love, our thrilled exhaustion. I remember the softly spicy smell of the elegant body that loved mine and the moisture burnishing her pubic hair, and I remember watching, without telling Jill what was happening, a tremendous spider, its legs twice as extensive as one expects, making its way down the jamb of the bedroom door, the only omen I have ever seen.

SEVEN

THE FOLLOWING MORNING, when I telephoned Jill to declare myself in love with her, she reciprocated in full, and I had a brand-new, official girlfriend. Though she lived with her parents, her natural independence gave her almost complete availability. Jill made decisions. She knew what she was doing. She planned to break with Tom immediately, and I had no question that she would. Our choice of each other was so equally emphatic, we had come together so fast out of nowhere, with such force, that we made clean, inevitable-seeming sense. We both knew what we were doing. What had happened spoke for itself. We could not fail to stick and grow.

Jill's emphatic nature—her speedy walk, determined and short-stepped, like a sewing machine; her frequent, gurgly laugh; her impatience, disgust with banality; her directness; her interest in what she experienced—assured me that I had chosen well, that she stood for everything more than sexual delectability, that she was "a person." I had come a long way from Margaret—I could choose someone juicy, and lacking intellectual "prestige"—but I still needed to be able to tell myself that the woman of my choice was altogether important, major, implicitly final. Given the chance, I scorned "playing around." Jill had less wit by far than Lizzie (where Lizzie mocked, Jill hated), and far less information or originality than Lizzie; but she was, this vivid and independent girl, *there*. I had someone now of my own. And someone I wanted to dare to invest with my entire body.

So—she broke with Tom—we began. We went to the theater, concerts, the opera, and to bed. At the box-office, Jill was able to find certain seats in the balconies of Carnegie Hall and the Metropolitan Opera that I could get into from my wheelchair, saving me, or us, important amounts of money and giving me an expanded sense of my flexibility. I knew by now that my muscles had grown back as far as they were going to, that the quantity of basic strength I could call on in my new life had been completely established. But I "knew," too, that I had not finished learning what it would be possible for me to do with my body within its certain limitations, thus that my recovery was not finished. My ambiguous condition, my extreme confusion of paralysis and strength, of independence and dependence, the limbo state of my body—useful leg muscles and unbalanceable back; clumsiness and refinement in my arms and fingers; my full energy and endurance and my wheelchair; my imperative need for the chair and the ease with which I could get out of it into a car, a theater seat, onto a toilet seat, a bed, upstairs—the mélange of possibility and impossibility I contained made my future mysterious. I had stopped having the bladder infections that had recurred over the new life's first three years. I had moved off the bedpan; at some point, I was sure, I would be discarding the enema rig that stood beside the toilet like an intravenous pole. And I knew that my penis would become more dependable, maybe dependable. Who knew? But I knew.

With Jill I became reaccustomed to desire. When I wasn't with her, I had her undressed in my head, as if she were an overwhelming compliment I could not stop reviewing. When I was with her at a theater or a table or in a taxi, I would look at her legs and think of them spread, of their lathed fineness; of her charming bush; of her nifty breasts; of her almond cream odor. She was a daydream, the ideal adolescent for a rapist who cares whom he rapes. In bed with her in fact, I grew erections regularly. I would crawl across her, like a soldier in maneuvers, and manage to raise myself up by elbows and hands. But my arms would collapse before I could enter her fully; or, if I had entered, before we could get a rhythm going; or I would wilt in her, or while nudging my way in. On occasion, I was too big to enter her. Several times, the skin of my penis split in a pin-thin line of blood. I wasn't near to coming in her and couldn't, without using my tongue or fingers, bring her to coming. But I loved using my tongue on her. I licked her with the contentment I had imagined when I'd met her; I licked luxury. In her mouth, I was my least firm, and she could accomplish nothing with me by hand (as I had not been able to myself, since the accident). I was elated, though, at my distinct advance, and we were glad of the comfort of our intimacy. To feel like failures would have been beside the point. We kept at our mechanics, but we had no deadline, and nothing to prove. Except the need, evidently, if we were going to do it, to "do it right." It didn't occur to us that Jill and I should switch positions. I must have felt that to lie on my back would be to "give up" to my weakness. So I poked and stumbled in the wrong direction, while behind us normally muscled men basked supine, and their pumping partners thrived.

Jill's general effect was to make me feel as if I were uncrippling. It soon emerged that the effect of her love for me on her father was to make him feel that she had disfigured him by throwing acid in his face. He had sat in a car with her, she told me, and wept, "You're in love with a cripple." But Jill and I were not going to let her father succumb to shame on our account. We went to her parents' for dinner. They entertained us civilly. The situation was a lesson for me in the contours of politeness. Jill's father had sobbed over her love for me; he had called me, in effect, a body-nigger; but he and I talked almost as if we felt no reason to fear each other. He was nervous as if on my behalf: wouldn't I be more comfortable eating off a tray set across the arms of my wheelchair than off the table? His wife reproved him—Dick knows what he's doing, Harry. He did not come across to me as the enemy he was until—when Jill and I were talking about *West Side Story*, the musical, which we'd just seen and admired—he said he'd disliked it because it was so tragic and ugly, and "you didn't have to go to the theater for that." From the right distance, I could have found this particularly repulsive cliché, with its chord of stupidity, stinginess, and fear, an entertaining surprise; one doesn't expect to hear it said. But I was up against the man who'd said it. I might, conceivably, persuade him to stop weeping over his daughter's love for me, but after I'd done that, I would only hit rock.

In early winter, Doubleday's immense benevolence called me into her office. I had "been seen," she told me, with the pride one shows as the bearer of good news, on the street in front of the office by the Director of the Catholic Textbook Division, and he wanted me to work for him. Her announcement made me feel like the winner of a Salvation Army beauty contest, but I didn't challenge her, or the textbook Director's, milky gaucherie; I only tried to make sure, with as much tact as I could find on the spot, that working in Catholic Textbooks would be another phase of my training and not a permanent job. I wanted badly to get "upstairs," meaning the general editorial floor. So it was important to take the Catholic Textbook assignment without complaint, and without questioning the peculiar nature of its origin. I'd had enough of the flap-copy department. Jacket-writing is almost inevitably controlled by cliché, so in one important sense it was not a job to be taken seriously; and I was being asked to take it seriously by people whose livelihoods depended on its being taken seriously. The staff worked very hard pumping air into leaking tires. This was not, in the familiar complaint, what I had gone to college for (and not gone to graduate school for). Catholic Textbooks had the virtue for me of being a change, if that's all it would be.

My job was to write reports on the competition, say a sixth-grade parochial school social studies book. The Catholic propaganda I encountered in my reading was too silly, and not hostile enough, to be interesting or more than irritating; and I was not, in any case, being asked to alter the slant of Catholic education. In fact, I had no motivation for the job at all. I dawdled, or I spurted ahead and finished a day's work quickly. I spent most of my time doing Double Crostic puzzles. No one seemed to notice. I did enough work to get by, but not enough to make a conspicuous impression.

Upstairs on the 17th floor, where I wanted to be, the glamorous editors of the company resided, producing books written by writers you'd heard of, and sold in bookstores (not, dimly, by mail-order or to schools) and advertised in the papers; doing the work that to my mind had the most color and importance, and would mean the most to me to do, as a prospective writer. I was eager to put out books on the way to putting out one of my own; I had begun, most cautiously, a novel about a young man who falls down a flight of steps and breaks his neck. And I was, as I had been from childhood, peculiarly interested in backstage activity. At eight or nine, I had been given a miniature stage, with drawable curtain, lights, and other equipment; in the basement, I'd designed and lit sets for this toy, working for entire days, thrilling myself. As an early adolescent, going to the theater, I went backstage after the show as often as possible, to enter the wings, to stand in what felt like the place of ultimate mystery, the secret source of reality, a room one doesn't belong in, like one's parents' room. My two seasons as an apprentice in summer stock, at sixteen and seventeen, had exhausted my wish to be an actor, but they had allowed me to live at length in the world that made the world, to tiptoe around in the dark brain of the stage, pulling the ropes and levers the audience couldn't see that controlled what they saw and watching the performers solemnly prepare themselves to go out into the public light. I had a few small parts myself during the two summers, and it excited me to get them and absorbed me to perform them. Absorbed me: once I was onstage, I'd given up my powerful, dreamer's view from the wings of the relation between backstage, stage, and the stage of audience; I'd left the incomparably crucial scene. I have always, with a devout kind of nosiness, had to get behind human atmospheres, acts, statements, gestures, styles, to explore safety for danger and danger for safety, to locate and take hold of "truth," cause, motive, origin.

I'd visited the 17th, the backstage, floor at Doubleday frequently during the course of my flap-copy stint, or to see a friend. At some point I'd discovered that the entrance to the men's room up there involved two doors, at right angles, separated by a foyer that appeared to be no bigger than the wheelchair. I began to worry—I once dreamed—about the men's room doors. If I got promoted to the editorial floor, was it possible I'd have to decline the promotion because I couldn't get into the men's room? Would I not get promoted because they knew I couldn't get into the men's room? I would not be valuable enough for them to permit me to work from an office on another floor, inconveniently out of the editorial flow. If I couldn't move to the 17th floor, were I asked, what would be the point of staying at Doubleday? If I stayed in publishing, I wanted only to be an editor. What other company could I go to, with no training? For that matter, what would the entrance to the editorial men's room of another company be like? I decided I had to risk learning whether I could get through the doors. I went up to the floor one day with no other purpose. As if I were heading toward business, I wheeled past the receptionist and into the hall. I aimed the right foot-rest of my chair at the necessary angle and shoved open the first door. I drove the chair three-quarters of the way into the tiny foyer. I tried to nudge the inner door open, but there was not room enough to turn the chair sufficiently to open the inner door while it was fully closed. I did not know whether there would be room to turn even if the door were fully open. I stayed there, stuck, like a car that has rammed a tree, until an editor came along. He leaned over me and pushed the inner door open. I jerked the chair leftward, straightening its direction, scraping the door, and I bumped over the threshold into the men's room, feeling as if I had reached a meadow. I would have to wait for help, in and out, but my relief overwhelmed the thought of such inconvenience. My anxiety had been reduced by nine-tenths: I worried now that I would not be asked up because it was known that I had *difficulty* entering the men's room.

Doubleday, like most of the world, did not see me as the unrequested bother I could imagine myself to be, did not see me as importantly queer. In the spring of 1958, I moved upstairs to become a "reader," that is, to read unsolicited manuscripts and to contribute judgment concerning manuscripts under consideration. I was given a ten-dollar-a-week raise (my second) and a private office, the manuscript storage room.

The trainee garden was being weeded. At just about the time I went upstairs, Cal was fired; he planned to leave New York. We had maintained adequately smooth relations, never moving beyond acquaintance-like conversation, never doing things together. We neither liked nor disliked one another. It was the rent-sharing I would miss, and required. But I didn't want a new roommate, I wanted a new apartment I could afford alone. For something like six weeks I was on the phone every morning for as much as an hour, the apartment-ad pages of the *Times* spread before me on my Doubleday desk, telling my peculiar problem to more or less uninterested real-estate agents and superintendents, seeking an affordable apartment with no steps at its entrance. (My father had said he did not want me living alone in a building without some personnel on the premises. In my phone inquiries, I censored this additional requirement.) I could not find the necessary combination. The money I would be able to pay—under a hundred dollars a month—usually got one a walk-up, or an oddity on an obscure, taxiless street, or a place outside Manhattan that, if I lived there, would heighten the cost of taxi transportation to the level of a rent I couldn't afford. I looked at only one apartment, a room with kitchen and bath, ideal building, two hundred a month. The city had never seemed taller. I was saved, eventually, by a friend whose parents were friendly with the owners of a large number of mellow apartment houses, many of them rent-controlled. I jumped a waiting-list and arrived at a staffed and stepless building on a taxi-rich street. The super showed me to a large, empty, sunny room with a small kitchen I could enter and a bathroom I couldn't.

The bathroom of the apartment I'd shared with Cal had been so small that even though I was unable to get my chair through the door, I had only to stand up and I could sit down on the toilet. Here, after a six-week search, in just the apartment I needed, its rent ninety-seven dollars, the bathroom door was too narrow for the chair, and the toilet and sink were steps away. I had no choice but to make the bathroom possible for me. Otherwise, I would be choiceless. In a headlong improvisation, I locked the chair in the bathroom's doorway and stood up. I grabbed the towel rack I saw at my right, and the steam pipe to my left. I took a tiny step with my left leg, and another with my right, and another with my left. I let go of the towel rack and reached for the edge of the sink with my right hand. I grasped the sink's edge, and, letting go of the steam pipe, pivoted, and sat down on the toilet. I nodded at the super, standing behind my chair. I pushed up on the sink, at my right, and the bathtub, at my left, rose, tipped forward, grabbed the steam pipe with my right hand, then the side of the doorway with my left, took a step sideways, pivoted, and sat down in the chair.

My parents were away on vacation when I found the apartment. I wired them the news. I learned later that they were so sure I would end up having to find a new roommate, instead of finding an appropriate new apartment, they hadn't worried about my wanting to live alone. But once I found a place, the right place, evidently they stopped worrying. My parents, as always after the accident, let my motivation lead. In August, I moved, with spare furniture from their house.

If my parents had ever disapproved of a girl I'd approved of, it would have been more on my behalf than on theirs. Lizzie's mother wasn't worried first about Lizzie, or Jill's father about Jill. They were worried first, it seemed clear, about family reputation, family satisfaction. However much I meant to their daughters could not make up for what I meant to *them*. My far more flexible parents understood the flexibility of experience—knew that it was the exception when what seemed jibed with what was. They had a higher (though not limitless) regard for the value of experience as such; also a shrewder sense of the finiteness of experiences. They were usually able to let the course of a matter speak for itself, as they had done when I sought, then found, my own apartment. If I, in a wheelchair, had fallen in love with a young daughter of theirs, they would have asked questions, or waited to see what happened. They would not have decided who I was without knowing me. They would have looked first at me and their daughter in relation to one another, and perhaps at me in my relation to my wheelchair. They would not have started and stopped with the wheelchair itself and them.

It was also true that my father, over the years, had had very little to do with me and my girlfriends. If he met them at all, it would tend to be accidentally. My mother was a confidante: I stuffed her ears with beginnings, middles, endings of love. She had more patience than my father would have, and also, like many mothers, she had more tolerance for sexual news, "even though" she was a woman. But she expressed judgments about my choices and actions little more than my father did.

At twenty-five, five and twenty, I wanted more parental recognition of sexual life, my father's recognition in particular. I wanted him to see the women I saw. A few years after the accident, he had ruminated to me his concern that my new life might not provide me with enough experience. I wanted to show him otherwise. Women were a way of showing him. I brought Jill up for a weekend, that is, my mother met us in the city and drove us up. Jill and I didn't need a place to go to bed together; I brought her home because she was a serious girlfriend, because I wanted to show her off and show her around. My bed was still set up in the dining room. Jill and I got cozy for the night. My father, coming home from a drive somewhere, entered the house through the dining room's French doors, though he could as easily have come in through the kitchen door or the front door. Jill and I called hello to him from our bank at the edge of the moonlit darkness, and my father, passing through, gaily said goodnight to us and went on upstairs. I felt married to Jill and married to my father.

Jill and I and my father went to the opera together one afternoon, *The Abduction from the Seraglio*, at the City Center. When the performance was over, before I got out of my seat, I put my coat over my lap and urinated into my portable pot. I was startled to hear, from both Jill and my father, flustered disapproval: what are you doing? Can't you wait? Both of them knew as well as anyone that once I had to urinate, getting out of my seat first and into my chair, and up the aisle and into the men's room, would lose me my retention. They must have been embarrassed in front of one another. I felt betrayed by each of them. But the day could not be spoiled. Before we left the theater, my father suggested we go to that night's opera, Verdi's *Macbeth*. He bought three tickets. We had dinner and came back.

I should by now have expected Jill to show embarrassment over my urinating at the opera while in my seat, no matter how privately I did it, but I was trying to duck the knowledge that her impatience (once known as precocious conviction) could turn on me. Irritating her was additionally hard for me to anticipate because what provoked her I had come to think of as a rough definition of virtue itself: my adaptive physical improvising. If I detained theatergoers as I got into my seat, Jill darkened and tightened, while the detained theatergoers couldn't have been calmer. If I urinated while on the street (in an empty doorway, the act concealed), she behaved as if I had done something foolish or dangerous, as if I had *tried* to embarrass her in public. Once, when I was slower than usual getting into a taxi, her anger came out so hot that after I left her off at her house, and was on my way home, the taxi-driver spoke of her tantrum incredulously.

Her impatience toward others had changed color for me. When she condemned a performance as amateurish, I had begun to think: she is too young, and too angry; *she* is amateurish. When she was disgusted with someone's stupidity or rudeness, instead of agreeing with her right off, I might now examine the stupidity or rudeness to see whether I thought it warranted her reaction. It had begun to appear, over the year and more of my knowing her, that Jill saw ineptitude, stupidity, and indifference in much greater amounts than I could add up. She was surrounded by insufficiency. If, before, I had allowed myself to decide she had few friends because she was so individual, independent, now it was worrisome to realize no one was good enough for her. When she was at my house, and the phone rang, she sulked. When she made a remark or presented an idea that I, with my own focusing irritation, found baseless, and I challenged her strictly—what do you mean? what does *that* mean? *then* what?—she wept. Her power was paling to frailty.

Again and again, my brain studied the film of the spider making its way down the door jamb on the first night Jill and I were alone. The insect had been warning me that romantic love wouldn't "work," that I was adoring Jill too rapidly, inflating her. I refused to believe the message. I might be a sucker for a dramatic symbol, but I knew better, after all; I knew that the spider was an accident, and symbols weren't accidents.

But if I knew better, I had to ask myself whether Jill herself was not a dramatic symbol, a romantic object, and I a sucker for her—even though it was as a romantic object, sexually, that she survived with the most strength. And if I stared too hard at the changed color of her temperament, wouldn't I leave her, or force her to leave me? I didn't want to do either. But her impatience was making me unhappy, and if she was impatient with me she was unhappy with me. Or just unhappy; but that was no help.

I went to a psychiatrist, a family friend. I asked him to tell me: did I want to leave Jill? I gathered that he rather thought I did. But I didn't have in me the instinctive certainty that had unstuck me from Margaret. Asking someone else what I wanted to do meant to me that I might still be in love.

By the early months of 1959, Jill and I were actively beginning to untie ourselves. Our dissatisfactions were increasingly direct. It would take longer for us to make up and less long to fight again. I finally admitted to myself that if I didn't trust her anger then I didn't trust her, and that whatever was admirable about the anger didn't make its source less destructive. She tore down the world because she feared its height. I couldn't join her rubble. As I had blurted love at the beginning, I did not try now to hide the symptoms of my disappointment: sourness, a floating distance, a failing of the energy to encourage her, or us. On an evening in late April, she quit, slamming my door. Immediately, I put my hands beneath the edge of a large table, and overturned it. With the crash, she came back, using her key. When she had helped me right the table, she left again. We had finished, but not quite.

Two days later, in the afternoon, I got a phone call from my brother. Dad was in the hospital. An aneurysm in his aorta had ruptured. I should come fast. In the taxi, I sobbed nervously, one shudder's worth. When I first went into my father's room, he apologized with intensity for having forgotten to send on to me a letter from a friend that had been mailed to my parents' house. I was holding my father's hand. I could smell him; he was soiled. He told me he had insomnia—he hadn't slept for ten minutes. Abruptly, then, he told me to leave, he had to vomit. I spent the next two hours in the hall and the waiting room. I had no idea what was happening, except that he had gotten worse. He and my mother had been driving to an afternoon dress rehearsal of an opera, *Turandot*, at the City Center, and on the highway he had felt sick. They had come to the hospital in an ambulance. At some point, in the hospital hall, I asked my father's doctor what was happening and the doctor said it was "all over."

When I was called in again, I didn't realize that he was actually dead. The room was crowded with people, and so quiet it seemed as if the world's noise had stopped, a plug pulled out. My father's body was covered up to the neck. His mouth was open in a way that made him look as though he were asleep but angry. My mother, sitting on the bed, stroked his forehead, as if to comfort him. I asked someone, whispering, whether my father was "gone," and I was told yes. My mother was gazing at him, beginning to remember him.

When Jill read the obituary, she was so upset she wanted to come back to me. For a few days, we tried to join, but I didn't want to, and we fell apart for good. I received a condolence letter from her parents.

EIGHT

THOUGH IMPRESSED by the size of my father's death, I missed, at first, the father rattled by my having to urinate while in my seat at the opera rather than the ebullient father who had taken me and Jill to the opera twice in one day; the father offended at the odor of my shit rising from the dining room, not the father who had invested himself with crucial vigor in my recovery. I missed the father who had bothered my poem with his ignorance, not the father who, over the years, had admired an original phrase and seen the point of a peculiar image. I missed the interfering anxiety, irritable dogmatism, self-involvement, petty paranoia, intolerance, domestic fussiness, the morning and evening rages, the oppressive government of the ogre who could seem to occupy the entire house, squashing the rest of us; and I missed the power that reached beyond the house as many miles as I had ever been beyond the house—that had kept the camera around my neck in Paris.

It did not hurt me that he had died at sixty-two, with his brain so busy, his concentration so taut, that he might have been starting medical school, when, in fact, he was retired. I did not mourn the intelligence intense to the point of seeming, to me, angry; his creative fascination with brains, rocks, turtles, birds, trees, with natural connections, with the natural nervous system; his alertness to the potential value of a reticent, or an obvious, detail; the sophistication of his judgment in refusing, or accepting, face values; the gleam of his professional and personal reputation; his charm; the comic sense I had hopefully played to; his prized tenderness; his scrupulous loyalty and courage. Both his parents had died when over a decade younger than he was at his death; he himself had been only fifty-four at the time of his first heart attack; my mother had been ill with asthma, sometimes perilously, on and off from 1937 to 1951, when she started using Cortisone; and then I had made a crater in his life. None of this calamity or strain subdued him. He took tragedy for granted without ever allowing himself to wilt, and he took danger as challenge. The most defeated he could be was frustrated. The last word he said alive—it could barely be understood—was "adrenalin." I knew no father who tried so hard to penetrate, who penetrated, as much of life as my father had.

He had died on a Saturday. On Monday, I was in the office, receiving sympathy as if it were acclaim. At the memorial service, the next day, not a tear dropped out of me. I was, rather, as tough —and must have been as pale—as ice; I was told I looked sick. I remember feeling as if my head might split from pressure. But I wasn't grieving. I was preserving my relief, had hardened it so that it couldn't dissipate. Or I had frozen my turmoil. My father was cremated.

At work, by now, I was being given projects and authors of my own to handle; I attended the weekly editorial meetings; I was consulted, my time was requested; people twice my age depended on me; I took writers to lunch at first-class restaurants— no more representations from the wheelchair baseball team; my phone rang all the time; I corresponded with Europeans. I rolled through days and nights so filled with work, responsibility, sociality, that I forgot my crippledness. My salary had gone up again. I was virtually self-supporting. I lived in my own cozy, colorful apartment. I was, very slowly, organizing my novel out of some of the stories I had written at home and at Columbia. "The life." If my father had been alive, the life would have been no different. It was my life. But I associated its lushness (what I thought of at the time as lushness) with an increased space and an improved soil my father's departure, and cremation, had seemed to leave me.

I could be lonely—feel high and dry. Jill was gone, too. For the first time in any kind of life, I wanted to be not in love but simply to be loved; or, if this is what a child wants, then I wanted it again. I had reason now, for the first time, to assess being in love, myself in love. Margaret, Lizzie, Jill. I needed to stop trying for a while.

I had a series of dreams of sexual tenderness. They were soft punches that left me stunned all the next day; yet I couldn't recognize the person I was dreaming about. In my notebook, in a "Closed Letter to One, Two, or More Women," I wrote: "What I want most of all is to be received by you." The likeliest "you" was Nora, a young woman at the office, but when I was out with Nora, a few times at a bar, a few times at dinner, once at the opera, the only excitement I felt was the excitement of not being able to tell her my dreams, which contrasted so mysteriously with her evident lack of sexual self-awareness. For me to have turned my yearning day-side out to Nora would have alarmed her. She was too passive to be the woman in my dreams, or to be told that she might be. She talked to me about her passivity—her general passivity—as a problem that concerned her, but not as a problem that concerned her in relation to me. Such talk was the closest we got. In my passion to be received, it may be that, dreaming, I translated her passivity into an abstract convenience. It may be that the person I couldn't recognize was my father disguised, or my husbandless mother. Whoever it was, or wasn't, I couldn't locate my love, asleep or awake.

Wanting most of all to be received by women meant, on the ground above my dreams, needing overwhelmingly to continue to know that women in the new world thought me attractive. With Jill gone (and my father gone), I used my sense of liberty to test my attractiveness. I became a Don Giovanni for whom a sexual conquest could be completed with the capture of an appealing woman's interest. Interest in me, or interest in me in my wheelchair? Interest in my transcendence of my wheelchair, I suppose; in my evident lack of self-pity, my stability, cheerfulness, humor, my "remarkable adjustment"; interest in my gaunt look, blue eyes, "sensitivity"; interest out of some identification with me, say with my differentness, or presumed "loneliness"; or interest out of curiosity, interest in me as "experience." What does he think about life from his unusual vantage point? He must be wise. He has suffered. I can talk to him. He will listen. (He has no choice.) What does his body look like?

I was greedy for interest but did not trust the interest I got. The interest did not see me whole, accurately, I feared. I feared being broken down into types. I did not give interested women time to develop trustworthy interest. I would disappoint them, or they me. I did not trust my greed, either, but I could not, did not think to, control it. I did not think of my greed as greed, and I must have felt, far beneath my behavior, that I was entitled to be greedy.

I fell in with Sally, a high school girlfriend of twelve years before. At the time, she had paralyzed my sexual muscles. I had never been able to move to kiss her, no matter how near she put herself to me. It was her nearness that had locked me. A magic weapon for her, her nearness. No matter how near she had put herself to me, I could not tell whether she wanted me to kiss her. And I'd had to know before I found out. I could not risk kissing her if I couldn't be sure she wanted me to. She had lost interest in me after a while, not surprisingly, but in the meantime she had not discouraged me, combing my hair as I lay in her lap, coming into my room, in her pyjamas and robe, when I once slept over at her house, to say goodnight. We had spent a lot of time together, and a lot of it alone.

Now, grown-ups, Sally and Dickie (as I had been known by her and a few others, still, at fourteen) went out some, cooked dinner for each other. She seemed to have lost nothing of the cheerful volatility that had captured me in high school; the vocal and physical animation that had brought me to the edge of sexual desire, where I would freeze. We chatted and laughed at top speed again.

A friend invited me to his country house for the weekend. I invited Sally along. On Saturday morning, she came into my room, to ask how I had slept. Come sit down, I said, patting my bed. She came and sat down. We had, then, a furious wrestling match for possession of her breasts. She said, "Gee, Dickie, I didn't know you were so strong." But I lost the match.

Her obstinacy, even if it expressed nothing more than her reasonable wish under pressure from my reasonable wish, revived the disturbing dilemma of my adolescence: feeling sexually provoked and sexually restrained—the dilemma that my amateurish marriage to unprovocative Margaret had seemed to crack.

I counted anger, adding to my anger at my sexual past anger at my recent life: at the flirtatious obstinacy of my crippled penis (I provoking, unprepared), at Lizzie's desperation, her mother's bullying ignorance; at Jill's pointless anger, her eventual acquiescence in her father's pathetic embarrassment. Into a strange room, its light the color of grapefruit, I pulled women I knew well, women I hardly knew, women I had merely seen, and I made them repeat their stupid remarks, their acts of sullenness, silliness, aggressiveness, selfishness, neediness, kindness, self-consciousness. I memorized their physical ugliness. I brought in my grandmother, now dead, and recaptured my rage at her feeble interferences. I thought of my mother in the year she'd borne me to and from General Studies; why had she had to look so exhausted from refusing to be put upon? I thought of women as vaginally offensive, of women walking as chafing, sweating, smelling; I thought of women running as stupid, women in groups as stupid, women laughing together as stupid. I thought of large breasts, like Sally's, as preposterous, as fatuous boasts.

A friend invited me to visit him and his wife in New Hampshire for a week of my vacation. I flew to Manchester. Since my flight to Nebraska, I had flown once again, to Washington, to visit Don Rahv, who was working there. (I would soon fly to his wedding, in Houston.) I liked to see myself getting myself out to the airport by cab; walking up the steps to the plane, holding the railings; walking to my seat, holding the tops of seats. I liked to see myself negotiating without much strain intricate acts of modern life difficult enough, yet also so much less difficult, for others. I liked experiencing my precarious flexibility, seeing it work, seeing myself at home one minute, at an airport another minute, in a distant city another minute. I had once been altogether unable to move.

My friend met me in Manchester and drove me to his rural house. His wife, whom I had not met before, was one of those people who impress you with their candor. When her husband was off doing something, she would pull up a chair and ask me, or conjecture at me, how I managed this or that, how this or that—not including such questions—made me feel. She interrogated me as if I had come to New Hampshire for advice about my physical life. As a week-long guest of a friend, I tried to answer his wife in a friendly way, but behind my mouth I hated her.

It was hot. I sat out on the scruffy lawn feeling baked to death. My sense of myself as dried up was so impressively intense, I tried to write a poem about it. In the poem, I asked that the sun burn me into wood, a piece of cherry wood, which a carpenter was to take and turn into implements—a music stand, a flute, a chair, a cup, and a plate. Big chunk of wood. Too big for a human poem. But trying—and failing—to write the poem turned out to be as important to me as it would have been had I finished a successful one. In acknowledging how high and dry I felt, how shelved, I saw at the same time that the feeling was no more than a piece of myself, the piece of wood big enough to make a music stand, flute, chair, cup, and plate—a dead body's legacy of objects useful to others—no more than a fat splinter. The poem was so awkward, I knew soon that I was not going to be able to finish it. I wrote three increasingly clumsy drafts of a beginning. The poem was not meant to be finished, or not in the solemn form I had imagined for it. Possibly as a two-line poem, as a metaphor alone, it would have had merit. Two lines for a fat splinter. When I got back to New York, I felt livelier, as if I had left the splinter behind me, for my friend's wife to whittle.

Over the next year, I went to bed with women who wouldn't have sex with me, or women I wouldn't have sex with. Gwen gently made it clear she wanted to fuck, was not interested in a tongue or a hand instead. There she lay, lovely. I cried at the pale blue of her nightgown, and didn't remove it. I didn't love her. I told myself, I didn't want sex with someone I didn't love. If I wanted sex without being in love, I didn't want it with Gwen, whom I liked enough to want not to fail with her. I felt I could afford to fail—not to keep it up, as if "keeping it up" defined pretense in me—only with someone I loved, or with someone who made no difference to me at all, whoever that could be.

Joyce wanted to wait until we knew each other better. What was the rush? she asked. I didn't know, but I couldn't wait. She was too stupid to wait for. But not too stupid to rush into. It didn't make sense. If I waited for her, I would be done with her as soon as I had had her, or as soon as I had failed. And I would have failed. I quit. Barbara wanted to "wait" for her husband. But her tremendous breasts were mine to do with whatever I pleased. Barbara offered me her breasts with the same force she used in defending her crotch. We writhed about, I a rolling pin to her dough.

Carrie, from the office, and I went for a weekend early in the summer of 1960 to Fire Island, traveling on a train, on a ferry. Our hosts were Dick and Margot Marek, who had been high school friends of mine, and husband and wife for five years now.

The Mareks and I were becoming new friends in our new lives. I had last been on Fire Island nine summers earlier, with Marek, a few weeks before he'd gone one way, and I another, to college for the first time.

Margot put Carrie in the room next to mine. When the house had quieted down (there were other guests), I went to Carrie and invited her to join me. She came into my bed and there told me the very long story of her very short marriage, how on her honeymoon her husband had chased women. Fighting sleep with one hand, with the other I would reach for Carrie, under the pretense of consoling her. She reacted in alarm, each time, and continued to talk about the man who had hurt her so badly, until I could no longer stay awake. Instead of declining to come to bed with me, she had come to bed with me to tell me why she didn't want sex; she had come to bed with my ears.

Deborah was sixteen, a maiden, a poet's dream. Certain dreams should remain dreams. I, by now twenty-seven, was astonished, once I learned of her age, that she would respond to me beyond blushes, absolute innocence, or fear. We were soon naked and playing. She wouldn't fuck, not because she hadn't, but because she had, the year before, unpleasantly. Deborah wanted to keep right on snuggling and playing, and gazing at me. Her eyes took time I almost immediately realized I had no wish to spend. She was bald need. A swarming nervousness as to what to do with this dream replaced my amazement and joy at having landed it. Ideally, I would have thrown it back, as undersized. But Deborah was neither fish nor dream, in fact. I wanted to say to her: "You were so desirable to look at from a distance, a painting of a girl standing alone in a room far down a corridor. When I learned how young you were, the thought of achieving you thrilled me. Achieving you dissolved the achievement. You could not survive once I touched you." But my change of feeling was not of the type I could comfortably explain; explanation could only embarrass each of us. I yelled at her, finally—at the real Deborah—to go away. Stop gazing at me. Be grown up. Be like me, realistic.

A few months later, at a party, I sat across a small room from a more womanly girl, who was giving me the eyes: steady, double-barreled desire. She was classical collegiate-literary, with the characteristic portals of dark hair. We said little to each other, but when the party started breaking up, she made sure I knew she was coming with me. Once in the taxi, we kissed so hard our teeth knocked. We had hardly known each other for perhaps three hours. When we got to my house, my bed, we undressed as immediately as we had kissed. I on my back, with my legs flung apart, my prick sprouted, she fit herself onto me. I held stiff, maintaining connection as she slicked me, until she came. I didn't come. A flare-up of boiling in the hips, and the boiling died. But I had held. I had done, nearly, what everybody did. I had done it by indulging my back, making a hammock of my weakness, subsiding into my abnormality. It was true: in the morning, Carla and I screwed again. She phoned her roommate, to check in, answering questions with happy, sliding hums.

Sometimes time seems to have been working privately for us, to have sought us out, waited for us in a particular spot, carrying a change of circumstances. Carla was time. Carla—not Margaret, not Nicole or Vaso, not Lizzie, not Connie, not Jill, not Nora or Sally, Gwen, Joyce, Barbara, Carrie, or Deborah, nor others I had in my new life kissed, felt, licked, stirred; tried, tried not, wanted, wanted not, to fuck. Why Carla? Why was *she* time? We didn't last three weeks. She drooped around the edges, showing herself to be—as someone just out of college commonly is—half-baked: grandiose but egoless, humorless but clever. Carla did something more important for me than springing my penis. If I would not love her because she had brought me down off the shelf, then I had not failed to love others because my penis had failed them. In sexual trouble, I was not reducing myself to sexual patient, nor rating women as sexual therapists. Yet now, after Carla, it seemed to me that, though I wouldn't love a woman because she'd cured me, I would not be able to pour myself into a woman unless I loved her; or else why, with Carla, had I remained dry? I needed time to come again.

One afternoon in my dormitory room at Columbia, I'd listened to Berlioz's *Romeo and Juliet Symphony*. The second part, *Great Festivities at the Capulets'*, when the lovers meet, is music of the most ferocious kinetic triumph; it seizes the space one occupies and flings it about. I pounded time on my desk, my shoulders danced. As soon as the *Great Festivities* had finished, I telephoned my father. I told him how the music had thrilled me, how glad I was to be alive, how exciting it was going to be to live. My father, sweetly enough, told me to take it easy, as if I had said to him that I knew I was going to get up one day soon and spin on light feet, as if I had developed a quack optimism. Four or five months after his death, I was listening to the Berlioz *Requiem,* on my phonograph. I went into my kitchen, to get something from the refrigerator. As I shut the refrigerator door, I sobbed. Instantly, I stopped sobbing. One sob. One sob had been the extent of my explicit grieving. More than a year later, I was still refusing to acknowledge my father's death as a loss. I would not let go of my dictator. Or I could not. I still behaved at him. I still behaved at him as I had for most of my life.

In the early summer of 1960, a member of the Doubleday brass had taken me to lunch and told me there was a chance I was going to be fired. Or I might be kicked upstairs. I would not accept being kicked upstairs, of course, I told him; why might I be fired? Disagreements with your superiors, he told me. I said to him that if I were to be fired, I wanted him—he was the person of high rank at Doubleday closest to being a friend and closest to me in age—to fire me. I probably felt he would fire me most honestly, most informally, with the least effect of paternal censure.

Disagreement with your superiors. This reason—the only reason given—could have been flattery. In the importance it gave (or lent) to my provocatively blunt editorial opinions, it allowed my friend-boss and me to avoid naming more intimate possible reasons, such as my terror and nearly servile good-heartedness in negotiating with authors' agents. The terror struck me blind whenever I had to look at a contract, and the good-heartedness came both from the terror—I wanted to get the negotiating done with as fast as I could—and from my instinctive loyalty to the author over the company. Well before I'd been taken to the warning lunch, I'd been chided, by a different superior, for being on "the author's side," as if I were the class fink. This loyalty, but more my ineptitude, cost Doubleday some unnecessary money.

My flustered resistance to the science of contracts and the science of money was all one with the science of shutting car doors and the science of driving cars, the science of gravity, the science of cameras, the science of brains, rocks, turtles, birds, trees. My resistance to contracts went back at least as far as second grade, when, unable to add seven and seven in front of the class, I'd cried instead; it went back to a high school biology exam, when, not thinking, I had written in penis, vagina, where I was supposed to write pistil, stamen. Flower parts were science and human sexual parts were sex. I resorted to more comfortable terms. On the leaf-investigating field trips of the required botany course at Middlebury, I stumbled persistently over the distinctions between monocotyledonous and dicotyledonous leaves. I flunked the required zoology course at Middlebury, because all I could do when I looked at a genetics chart was blink. Placed among "scientific" language I was a coward, bored and scared, lost, unwilling to find my way around. A contract, with its percentages and restrictions and pompous precision, was chaos, or science.

But fumbling contracts was only one way to make a mistake in such a complex job, among so many fathers, backstage, where it counted. The first book out under my editorship contained an elegant production error: a drawing, meant to illustrate text on the next-to-last page, appeared alone on the last page. I did not do the deed, but I failed to catch it. I wanted to sign Sir John Gielgud, my hero in London in 1951, and at the time doing a play in New York, to write a book. I received company permission to pursue the matter. Proudly "tapping a contact," I obtained the phone number of the apartment Gielgud was staying at. I was told to call early in the day and speak to Sir John's secretary. At the office the next morning, exactly at nine, I dialed the number. Gielgud himself, unmistakably, answered. I asked for the secretary. Gielgud, amiable to the brim, said the secretary was not in yet. I said thank you and hung up. It was not characteristic of me to be timid toward the famous. Why had I been so inopportunely tongue-tied? As if to find out, I went to *Books in Print,* the reference work any editor whose head is on straight consults before initiating non-fiction projects, and there I saw listed two books by Gielgud. I did not call his secretary.

My cowardice when faced with contracts, the clumsiness I could show in negotiation, the siding with authors—all was "disagreement with my superiors." But at that warning lunch, my friend-boss and I talked only about my tendency to be contemptuous of the commercial manuscripts under consideration, and my habit of deriding certain commercial manuscripts while recommending that Doubleday publish them. "This one stinks," I would conclude a report. "Probable best-seller." Good enough for you but not for me. I was unable to play the grown-up game of loving a book because a lot of readers might buy it. But I was unable, too, to play the grown-up game of moderating one's responses so that one wouldn't offend one's colleagues by scorning their jobs and thus expose oneself to joblessness. I could not resist trying to attract my male elders by embarrassing or irritating them, as much as I tried to please them.

In my defense, I had almost no supervision. I learned as I went. I could have made many mistakes I didn't make, and I didn't make many. What's more, I had brought in one pro-nounced commercial success. Since I had almost no super-vision, my superiors could know little about my editorial value. Authors reciprocated my loyalty, and my diligence. Dealing with problems in their manuscripts, I was confident, thorough, and imaginative. They trusted me, and they did their revisions for me.

In the late summer, a higher-ranking boss took me to lunch. We talked very little about the office. We talked like a father and son unable to talk, neither of us comfortable with anything the other brought up, because nothing we brought up was what we needed to talk about, and what we needed to talk about was too heavy to lift.

When I got home from work on November ninth, the day after Election Day, 1960—Kennedy triumphant, life on course again, a fresh wind in its sails, Nixon finished, at last, for good—I re-ceived a phone call from my mother. My mother told me that she had received a phone call from an acquaintance, acting on behalf of Doubleday, who informed her that Doubleday wanted to know whether I could afford to work there part-time, doing my own writing the other part of the time. Would Dick be able to manage? ("Can he get out of his chair?") Would the family situation permit it? My mother was firing me from Doubleday's employment.

I stayed calm while talking with her. I was so terrified to find her at the accident, I forgot I was in it. I remember saying twice that it made no sense for me to work there part-time because I had too much to do; why didn't they know how much I had to do? How could I do all that part-time?

From then on, the sound track is dead. I retain spurts of film. I am at the office early the following morning to catch the top boss, the man behind the intermediary, before his day surrounds him. I appear in the doorway of his wide office. He is alone, sitting at his desk. My arms flail. I yell at him (I remember the yelling but cannot hear it): why did you do this this way? If you wanted to fire me, why didn't you *fire* me? To my face! With these yelled words, I seem to have wounded him. He sags back in his desk chair. His arms hang. He gapes at me, dying, crumpled with pain. He apologizes: you're right. I know. I should have known. I'm so sorry. His niceness is notorious.

He hadn't been protecting me, he'd been protecting himself. It would have cost me no pain to be fired to my face; it was dismembering to be mishandled so gently. His brutal coddling has cost him, evidently, a lot of pain. He hadn't expected rage? Had he included it in?

For his part, I imagine the question to have been: how do we fire a nice young fellow in a wheelchair, bright, popular around the office, but whose space and salary can be far better used by someone with more ambition and loyalty and impersonal taste? If we fire him outright, and to his face, will he be able to take it? We are too decent to do that. Let his mother put it to him, someone who understands him. Not fire him, but make it possible for him to fire himself.

The bullet I have so suddenly become ricochets off the well-meaning top boss. I shoot to my friend-boss, as if on a murder spree. I ask him, why didn't *you* fire me, as we agreed? He says, what are you talking about? I tell him what has happened. I am so cleanly in the right, I'm thrilled; I'm scared they will unfire me. He rushes off to the top boss, and when he comes back clears it up, like that: the trouble was crossed signals, a breakdown in communications.

I have as much time as I want, on Doubleday, to look for another job. It is no problem at all for me to decide: I don't want another job. Nor do I choose to work "part-time," eat the insult. I will have severance pay. I will have unemployment insurance. And I will write my novel. And, of course, be rich then. I am a writer. No disguising it now. I should have quit Doubleday long ago, I begin saying to myself. I was enjoying lunch too much, being consulted, people older than I depending on me—mere ego-perquisites. The formal work on manuscripts I performed so well I should have been performing exclusively on my own manuscript. Doubleday says they want me to write. There is not enough book yet to show them for a contract. For my hope's files, I request and get a meaningless memorandum from the Editor-in-Chief, which "confirms our understanding that you are going to show Doubleday a sample of the writing you propose to do after you leave Doubleday and that we will work out a contract along the lines outlined in your memo to me, if the book manuscript is one which fits into our publishing plans." Theoretical publication before pride. Am I playing them off against guilt? Could I succeed in doing so? If they sign up my book—and I am terrified they won't—will it be a further insult? A last stroke of the pussyfoot?

Now I became a person "winding up his affairs," and, as if acting this famous role made me feel better, I did it gaily, like a success. I am sure I was relieved that the issue had been forced, no matter how awkwardly. My friend-boss advised me to say, in my letters to authors and agents, that I had resigned from Doubleday in order to write. Fired, I should not complain. My first reaction to this advice—why should I protect Doubleday?— was brief. The suggested form was for my *own* protection. Showing bitterness would be more reprehensible than being fired. To dine out on your own defeat is more reprehensible than almost anything. It means no one else is supposed to eat. Even the dying are expected not to stain their visitors with bitterness. I wasn't bitter about being fired, as such; and I wasn't, in any case, tempted to narrate the details of Doubleday's cowardice and clumsiness in my letters. So I did as I was advised and conventionally lied.

At the end of November, I started staying home, to work on my novel, "the novel," as one's novel is called, with no choice but to write. Though it was my own home I started staying home at, not my parents' (now my mother's), it was, still, "home" that I had once strained to leave, as a matter of life or death, so that I could eventually become a citizen. So that I could pay taxes. But "home" again now, sent back, sent in, from downtown, from card-carrying membership in the crowd, I did not feel as if I were going to flake to death in the cozy vacuum. I felt nearly proper being there. It had tired me, scrambling daily to keep up with the life I had been so proud to reach, catching cabs, being on time, pushing myself through the thick daytimes and deep into evenings, without stopping. I had overproved my endurance. Effort and smoking had weakened my gums. They'd needed periodontal rescue.

I'd been "retired" at twenty-seven, but I accepted the new comfort of my life. I did not have to be frightened of it. I had not lost my muscles. If I'd been "out" I could go "out" again, to another job, some other job. Since I'd been out, I did not, either, feel disgraced at staying home to write. One is not supposed to feel disgraced at staying home to write. A book is its own justification, is work, dignified, admirable, enviable. But a book was not enough justification for me in my circumstances then, in my concern with how the outside saw me. For me, it was all right to be working at home because people knew, or I could tell them, that I had "worked at Doubleday for three years," and because, above all, I did not have dependency to fear. I lived alone. (My independence would keep me company.) I would be depending on myself, in fact, more heavily than I'd done in my years at Columbia and my years downtown. (In two ways at once, this increased self-dependence was part of the new comfort of my life. The need for help sometimes costs more in strain than the help itself can repay you.) When women came to see me, or I brought them home, they would find no companion, nurse, roommate, emerging from another room. No one but I would open my door. My bed was not a hospital bed anymore. The layout of my apartment was not elaborated to serve one handicapped, with bars, pulleys, sterilized air, medicines, whatever an anxious visitor might anticipate. My physical virtue— my having worked downtown, my autonomy at home—was my justification for staying home to write.

What I worried about most, at first, more than working at home, and more, even, than the problems of the novel itself, was the quality of my future. Going out only at night, no longer working in a large office, no longer taking another agent or author to lunch, I would be meeting fewer people, fewer kinds of people, fewer women; I would be engaging in fewer dramas, fewer potential dramas. Having lost my job, I had lost a chance to become professionally skilled, reputable, to impress a vocational mark in the earth. Where would the noise I wanted my life to make come from now? The book it was going to take me, in isolation, well over a year to finish? Suppose the book made no money or no splash? My father's concern at the possibility that my experience would be peculiarly limited, it disturbed me to recognize, might not have been an unnecessary concern, as I had been able to think downtown, but only delayed in its accuracy. With my return home this time, the distinguishing event of my accident seemed to me over, the ocean of echoes it had caused dried, my tour as heroic survivor concluded. I felt that what drama, what impact, I made in the future, what experience I achieved, was up to me as it had never been in either life.

NINE

IN THE EARLIEST YEARS of school, we did "Rhythms." In leotard, Miss Dudley, gray-haired, muscular as wood, directed us. A pianist plunked in a corner of the gym. "Rhythms" was aesthetic calisthenics, a warm-up of physical imagination. We imitated basic nature; we played wind, trees, grass, growing flowers—the sort of thing that parodists of progressive schooling seize on.

At some point during "Rhythms," the scarves came out. I adored the scarves. They were small sheets, really, and silk, or silklike. We draped them around us, or trailed them, or swirled them, or knotted them together. They were each of one color that would gradually develop into a relative of itself. A scarf bright green at one end would become chartreuse at the other; red would become pink; yellow, lemon; pale-blue, turquoise; orange, crimson; beige, brown; gray, black.

My colors since the accident are not different from my colors before. They are, rather, altered in intensity—up or down—from what they were. The subtle shift of these colors is a shift of lives.

Assuming I would have been fired—though fired better— had I not come to Doubleday in a wheelchair (and assuming I would have been hired had I not come to Doubleday in a wheelchair), I am as sure as one can be without having been there that I would have looked for another job and not gone home to write.

I would not have imagined, without the wheelchair beneath me, that I had enough to write about. I would have kept a notebook of observations, and ideas for stories and novels. It disturbs me like a dream of an actual failure, as if I had, in fact, missed the chance to become a writer, the chance to learn my hidden mind, that in a parallel life I wouldn't have dared to go beyond the notebook, or not far enough to finish anything, or not for years. What would have made me? My accident gave me permanent pause.

What kind of job would I have looked for? On my feet, at twenty-seven, how would I have been different, how different would I have been? Would I have gone to Doubleday in the first place? From what college? Had I not gone to Columbia, I might not have gone to Doubleday. If I had finished Middlebury, having missed the accident, I would have gone either into the army or, to avoid the army, to graduate school, in American literature. An academic specialty would have suited me fine—knowing in capillary detail something no one else in my family knew except by name. Graduate school, then the army. Then teaching. Teaching where? Academic life would have been too quiet for me, certainly where, as I suppose, I would have found a job. I would have come to feel that teaching, including literary scholarship, was not enough for me, that whatever conspicuousness I might have developed would have been too isolated to suit me. I would not have gotten a job on a star campus, but if I had I would not have been a star there. I was not a scholar anyway. Sitting would have made me restless. I would have wanted to move, be known, in a city. In its repetitiveness and in its imparting of superior information—in the handing down of a specialty semester after semester—teaching would have suggested age to me. I imagine that I would not have grown, as a young teacher, would not have changed shape, expanded my specialty, that I would have stayed stuck to my subject until I angrily ripped myself unstuck. I would have been imitating, still, had it not been for the accident. I would have imitated age and "academe"—tweeds, pipes—parodied myself without wit, done the conventional things until I had to punish the conventions: unnecessary meetings, little literary jokes, academic pettiness, vanity, and timidity. I would have had to learn, like everybody, to trust my self-hood enough to exert it. I think that then I would have left teaching.

For what? Where, in my panic, would I have gone? What I had decided to do about the army would have decided my future. In the army, after graduate school, I might have learned not to take up a professorial life once I was free to or because I had learned a specialty to profess. But how would I have survived the army? I couldn't tolerate Middlebury, army enough, where a fellow-student had sourly told me to "get a haircut or buy a violin"; where another had cursed me as a "world-beater" when, as a freshman, I gave the Varsity Show a New York-snotty review (and where, after the review appeared, a bunch of the show's personnel dragged me up a flight of stairs to a dormitory room to scream their resentment at me); where another, in the dining hall, had thrown a pat of butter at me, hitting my nose; where twenty-five dollars had been stolen from my desk-drawer; where I had been as much disliked as I disliked. I had never before felt enmity for a group, or had a group of enemies.

In the army, it could only have been worse, or so I felt. And there were, as a separate matter, rifles. In training, I would have accidentally shot or been shot by someone. My friend Marek tells me he had precisely the same fears—the fear of enforced living with people he would feel to be stupid or hostile, and the fear of a rifle accident. He tells me he never got over his distaste for many of his fellows, and that he feels he was on the whole disliked. He tells me that he loved learning to shoot a rifle, and that he loved getting into physical shape, the renewal and the testing of his physical skill. If Marek survived the army, I could have, too. As things were, I would, at some point, have had to join. Very shortly after the accident, in the hospital, I received my Selective Service classification of 1-A, with student deferment, having passed the army physical. The only disability I had to offer at the physical was an occasional attack of sinusitis. I still carry with me my subsequent invulnerable classification of 5-A.

My father would have talked me into the army, if not out of my terror, by asking me, in effect, who did I think I was? I would have known I was nobody yet. And, sniffing my academic future, I would have been indecisive enough about going to graduate school to say to myself, get the army over with now. From college, then, in 1955, I would have entered the army. When I came out, I would have, most likely, looked for a literary job (while, perhaps, writing, without finishing it, a peacetime-army novel). In my sophomore year at Middlebury, I had asked my father to get in touch with high-ranking friends of his in the literary business to see whether they would interview me for a summer job. In fact, a writer friend of my father's, who spent his summers in upstate New York, had arranged for me an apprentice job on a newspaper up there the summer before my freshman year. I traveled to the town, like Major Molineux's kinsman in Hawthorne's story, and rented a room in a boarding house. I visited my father's friend. The job was all set. The next morning, I went to see the editor of the newspaper. A pleasant enough man, he had never heard of me, did not know of the writer who had referred me to him, and had no job for me, not even for no money. He wished me good luck at Middlebury; he was an alumnus. I ran righteously to the writer's house and found him thrashing in bed with a huge fever that made it impossible, his wife explained, for him to talk with me. Summer theater. This writer, whom my father had paid to do some work for him, never did the work and never repaid the money. He has since become known for books about political skulduggery.

Rather than go home right away—to do what?—I hung around the local playhouse for a few days, though they didn't have a job for me either. Since I had decided, at the end of the summer before (my second in summer stock), not to try to become a professional actor, what harm could there be in looking in on the atmosphere I still loved more than any other, the drama surrounding drama? Acting meant dying to me, now. In a repeated vision, as persuasive as a nightmare, I'd seen myself having attempted a career as a professional actor, face down in a Broadway street, dead of failure. My talent would not be enough, or, if it might be, I lacked or declined the ambition one needed before giving over to what I saw at the time as the theater's peculiarly disorganized kind of fate. The stage, in effect, could crack at any moment. Actors needed always to be ready to improvise their own salvation. This was why, I felt, they were so good at enjoying themselves after a show. Every night was critical with the possibility of failure—a dead audience, a memory lapse, a colleague's missed entrance, a blown line, a malfunctioning stage doorbell; and every night stood for the over-all peril of the performers' lives—auditions leading to nothing, uncertain money, constant, deceptive intimacy. No one is more responsible than a professional performer before and during a show. But, I felt, people willing to expose themselves to such risk, such risk of unemployment and such risks of employment, must be irresponsible to their own survival. I feel this way now about racing-car drivers. I was worried most of all, I am sure, by my own proved capacity for carelessness. As prop-boy, during my first season in summer stock, I forgot to put a note on a tray to be brought onstage by a maid. The reading of the note by the master of the house—my father, a conscientious psychoanalyst would say, perhaps correctly—was crucial to the play's development. The actor, who happened to be the manager of the playhouse, and who had hired me, somehow faked it. I turned faint, was ready to go home for the summer. The following summer, at the end of which I decided to quit the theater, I was assistant stage manager during the production of a pre-Broadway tryout, in which Gertrude Lawrence starred. Gertrude Lawrence was standing beside me, watching the action, ready to make her entrance. Next thing I knew, she was on the floor, passed out. I pulled the curtain. I turned on the houselights. I turned off the houselights. I opened the curtain. I started up a phonograph record on a machine to my left, to divert the audience, and, putting on the needle, scratched the record, the scratch making a monstrous tin belch over the amplification system. I was only seventeen. Others in my shoes would have come apart, too. But others still would not have. All through my youth, I was in training for my automobile accident; I would not have had to be called, but I was ready. A writer has time and galleys in which to erase mistakes.

At some point, then, in a parallel life, in a life after I had not lost control of Mike's car, I would have become a writer, but a downtown writer. After the army, with or without graduate school, I would have joined a publishing house, or a magazine, or a newspaper, or each of these in succession, and perhaps in continuing succession, and would not have been good enough to make the job good enough for me, would not have shone. Eventually, I would have become professional at something literary downtown, but the more I became professional, the more I would have missed "seriousness," the chance to study my imagination, to become fully peculiar. Yet, I would have been too fragmented and too restless for seriousness, more restless than I can be in the wheelchair when I have more energy than I am able to use. I would not have been able to sit still long enough, keep my brain still long enough, to write a book; and I would have been able to avoid sitting still long enough to write stories. Never in either life, not even in the hospital, had I needed to get used to profound solitude. In a parallel life, at twenty-seven, I would not have risked staying long enough out of the sight of others to be able to write in a way that might explore the back of my mind, where the scenery was stored, where actors waited to go on. The accident—carelessness, finally, that I couldn't take back—forced me to learn, or allowed me to learn, several kinds of discipline, including prolonged concentration.

It was also as if the accident, in altering me, in throwing me into permanent conspicuousness, had insisted that I use the artist part of me—the third hand, which altered reality, fiddled with, rearranged, wouldn't let alone, imitated, parodied. As a baby, to my mother's chagrin, I jazzed up her bedtime songs. As a child, dressed in any costume, I was in awe of myself. To be about to go onto a stage in a school play when I was nine meant to me what it must mean to a rookie playing in the World Series, or to an astronaut about to touch the moon, or to a traveler reaching China for the first time. I had my toy theater to dress and populate. I was an adolescent actor onstage and everywhere else. At Middlebury, having turned "writer," safe from the death that acting had come to signify, I acted in several productions. At the start of my sophomore year, in the last of these, *Ring Around the Moon,* I played twin brothers of opposite temperaments, the ultimate moment for me of physical imitation, and got bravos from the campus where I had been as despised as I was despising. The Middlebury Drama Director (whose wife would soon be demonstrating the making of Christmas-tree ornaments to me and the other crippled patients at the Mary Fletcher Hospital) privately raised to me the idea of my playing Hamlet the following year. I would have done it; after all, I was half Hamlet already. I had almost always loved to stick out. I had almost always been successful, sticking out. Now I was sticking out by being at home, alone, at twenty-seven. A writer is a still actor.

I learned that it was easy, at home, for me to continue to make drama; and I learned—as if it were the kind of thing one has to learn—that drama meant trouble. If I needed to continue to make drama, I must have wanted, among other things—such as completing a novel, selling it, seeing it published; such as love, peace, pleasure, sexual restoration—trouble. It was as if, the accident "over," I had to make new catastrophes to maintain my reputation, as if my reputation for catastrophe were the only one I could bank on.

I telephoned a young woman who worked at Doubleday. We had passed a few times, quickly smiling, in the fish-tank corridors. I remembered her as small, slender, dark, soft-faced. I knew nothing else about her but her name. I wasn't at all sure she'd know who I was. But she remembered me, and was pleased to accept my invitation to dinner at my house. She was a painter, I discovered at the beginning of the evening, and she always went to bed with men whose pictures she painted or drew. She drew a picture of me. Her body smelled of turpentine. We had an adequate screw, in the terms that were, for me, adequate— I serving, in effect, as an accompanist. She slept over. In the morning, I wished never to see her again. She phoned a few times. I put her off until she stopped. A friend of her family's, it turned out, was a friend of my family's. In the course of a phone conversation, my mother casually reported to me, without any color of disapproval, that she had heard about a young woman who had been hurt by my abrupt retreat. I was forced to think, then: the girl must have wondered what she had done to me. I wondered: had I dismissed her because of her turpentine odor? Because she hadn't brought me along sexually? Would I have wanted to see her again if we hadn't gone to bed? Only until we'd gone to bed? If our sex had been more successful, what would I have done with the rest of her? All that interested me about her offended me—the motive and ease with which she delivered herself to bed, to beds, and her turpentine odor. I went to a party. There I met a young woman. I had a lot to drink. We left the party for a restaurant. At the restaurant I had another drink. I was all excited over this girl, voluble, urgent. I ordered sauerbraten. I looked at the sauerbraten and took myself out to the sidewalk, where I sat in the intense cold, hoping to freeze my nausea, while the girl ate her dinner alone. We went to my house. I was feeling better. Come to bed with me, come to bed. No, she said, she was involved with someone, had been for a long time, couldn't betray him. When she left, I was sober and gloomy. The next day, she phoned, wanting to come back. Come, I said. When she arrived, almost immediately she was taking off her clothes. I lay on the bed, still clothed, watching her from behind. Her ass looked like cottage cheese. She lay down next to me. I touched her cunt. Instead of wettening beneath my fingers, oozing satin moisture, she shot hot juice. I could feel the impact of a spurt, as if she'd had a vaginal ejaculation. No, I said; I don't want this. (Her violent need? Expressed as I couldn't express my own?) In pain, rapidly, without debate, she dressed and left. A close friend of *hers,* it turned out, was a close friend of my mother's. My mother, who had now been yanked into my life, by hands other than mine, for the third time in a few months—my firing from Doubleday and my firing of two women—phoned me, with the direct purpose, on this occasion, of telling me she had been told that I had dangerously upset (she named the name) by my contradictory and abrupt behavior. The girl's, and my mother's, close friend had suggested to my mother that I go to a psychiatrist. I shouted my rage: why had my mother been brought into the matter? Why hadn't her friend spoken to me instead of her? But, my mother quietly explained, the girl and her friend had been terribly upset. I described to my mother the girl's behavior, pointing out that it had been hardly less confusing than my own. My mother, having now heard more of the story, agreed with me. But, she said, the girl had problems, which I had stirred up.

I could not remember my mother ever having been so neutral before in her judgment of me; as a son, I had been either wrong or right. She was trying, now, to treat me as a friend. She was trying to indicate that I had reason to watch what I was doing, trying to show her concern without, like a mother, declaring it. Her concern was not only for me but about me. But a mother could not tell her son that he was being dangerous. But she could have told her friend to leave her out of it.

I was appalled by the accidentally interlocked unfairness of what had happened, my unfairness, the girl's, the friend's, my mother's, each of us helpless, each of us wrong. I felt myself to be stuck in the bars of the structure, and spotlighted by coincidence. The two girls, who didn't know each other, each had a friend. Both friends, as it happened, knew my family. (In neither case had I known of the friends from the girls, or of the girls from my family.) Each girl had complained about me to her friend. Both friends had passed on the complaints to my family; one complaint had come indirectly, one directly, to my mother. It was as if I were being punished, by being embarrassed, for punishing, humiliated for humiliating. (For picking up and dropping, as if I had caught myself shoplifting.) What was I doing? Why so harshly? Was I in a runaway panic, now, of sexual failure? I was frightened that if they were interested in me, if they stayed interested in me, I would be unable to get rid of them because I could not literally run from them or push them away. They were asking of me what I had asked of them and could not give them. The sense of love coming from the wrong woman (the woman who loved me?)—the woman I didn't want, didn't like, who was a mistake—panicked my muscles. I "loved" too quickly; I could not bear my characteristic mistake being committed against me. Did I imagine there was something wrong with women, as I had wondered of Lizzie, if they were interested in me? Was I seeking out the wrong ones for me, imagining I was unable to afford being loved, fearing the evaporation of myself? Or was I, rather, frantically seeking out a new Lizzie, a new Jill, and throwing aside women who wouldn't do? The answers to my questions, if there were any, if I was going to learn them, I wanted to learn through experiences, not consultation with a psychiatrist. I didn't want anyone telling me the story of my life.

I didn't want anyone telling me the story of my life, even though the psychiatrist I had consulted two years earlier, when hoping to learn whether I wanted to break up with Jill, had thrilled me with his explanation of a dream I had reported to him. In the dream, my parents and I (this was shortly before my father's death) were in a train with a lot of Communist Chinese, miserably trying to escape the fallout of an atomic bomb. The fallout's gritty odor, a smell of iron dust, was infiltrating the train. We were sick, weakening, doomed, as we tried to escape. The psychiatrist told me I was the bomb. The impact on me of this news was greater even than the hideous impact of the dream, and it was, for several reasons, great to the point of pleasure. I was so impressed with the secret he had told me, with its being simultaneously so astonishing and so inevitable, and so excited by being *it,* being the secret itself—being named Oedipus the King, the discovered author of a great play which is one's own life—that I swallowed the point right along with the pleasure. I understood the point, but it didn't hurt. In any case, I thought at the time that the bomb-hood the psychiatrist had conferred on me was retroactive, covering only the accident and its severest effects, that period in which I had been dangerous, to my parents, because my life was in danger or my future oppressive.

Now, two years after this beautiful revelation, and nearly eight years after the accident, I felt the point; the pleasure had melted off. I had learned not only that drama meant trouble, but that trouble meant *trouble*—that there was a difference between trouble on a stage and trouble off a stage. And I had learned not only that making trouble hurt others, but that, at the same time, it hurt me. My continuing explosions damaged me. I bombed myself. I couldn't have enough of this knowledge, evidently.

One morning in late winter, while I worked on my novel, I received a letter from Deborah, the poet's dream of the summer before, now at a university out west. Deborah's voice was cheerful and only charmingly, seductively wounded, when she reported that she was seeing a man even older than I. Age was no problem for her, she said. The letter's sexy unexpectedness and its cordiality excited me, allowed me to anticipate; and the intelligence of its style, firm and light, made my excitement respectable. The poet's dream (in less than a year!) had become a person my own age, someone it would be realistic of me to deal with, someone I could "talk to." But Deborah—so that she wouldn't scare me, she subsequently told me—had not provided her address. I wrote back that morning, as much as praying that "Freshman dorm," after name, university, city, and state, would locate her. It did. We wrote with multiplying frequency, and with increasing polishing of the sexual point, I, of course, explicit, doing my dramatizing, she less strenuous but as eager. It was as if nothing had gone wrong once. We spoke on the phone several times, like lovers missing one another, though we didn't declare love. She would come to see me the first day of her return to New York at spring vacation. I became worried that her period would coincide with her visit. She assured me that it wouldn't.

When I opened the door to her, we kissed, probably without saying hello; then I locked the wheels of my chair and stood up, so that we could press as we kissed. Then we went to bed. We did whatever we had done the year before—naked stroking and kissing, but no screwing—and after that we held each other, lovers reunited. I took in her look, the classic look of safety waiting for confirmation. I took it as a child's look, the look of a daughter about to be tucked in. I felt as if, without thinking, I had adopted Deborah. I felt, at the same time, flat. I had lost more than a month's worth of excitement in less than an hour. There was nothing to take its place but Deborah, gazing at me. Look, I said, are you in love with me? Yes, she said. I asked her, would you marry me if I asked you to? Yes, she said. Then I became flustered, as if she had said "I love you" or "Marry me." I said, but that's crazy, you don't know what you're saying, you don't know me, we don't know each other, I'm ten years older than you, don't you realize that? I don't remember her answers, only my panic, my sense that each of us was a fix that each of us had gotten the other into. With my frightened questions, I hammered her away from me. Again, Deborah left my house bewildered, punished.

She had written to *me*, but I had responded, urgently. I had not ignored her letter, or been able to respond to it as if it were not an invitation, or been able to avoid making my response an invitation, or written her that it would be best for us to keep our distance, considering the pain I had caused her. Maybe I had taken her letter as a chance to undo the pain I had caused her. But I had, then, injured her again, worse because twice; and even though she, like the two girls preceding her reappearance, had made it easy for me, I was the one who had done it because I was the one who could have declined to do it. If Deborah had wanted to fuck, and I had been fully able to—if we had been able to be sexual "adults"—perhaps I would not have panicked in bed with her. But I would have panicked shortly after; asked myself what I was doing. What *was* I doing? And why had I so scornfully, so vengefully, asked her questions that made it sound as if she were untrustworthy, as if she had seduced me? But I *couldn't* trust her, at her age; and she *had* seduced me. Why had she written? Why hadn't she stayed away? My victims insisted on me. I did not "know my own strength." I did not know strength. To be as dangerous as a bomb was to be weak; anything could set me off. I was not my own bomb.

In the parallel life of my junior year at Middlebury, with Margaret having transferred to Clark, I would have become, in my letters to her, a lonely lover urgently anticipating reunion, and we would have visited one another. We would maturely have suffered longing (longing for what?), suffered the sacrifice, the "hard work" adult love costs. We—I—would have done this suffering for perhaps three or four months. We did not need the accident to separate us; the accident kept us together a year longer, I would guess, than we would have stayed together without it. Margaret's transferring to Clark was not intended by her to separate us, as far as I know—as far as I was concerned, nothing could separate us—but, for my part (and it may be what she intended), suddenly without Margaret on our height of mature love, where the wind had been terrific and the oxygen sparse, once I had allowed myself to acknowledge my freedom and my wish for it, I would have descended to my age, at last, and scampered to sex. Imagining as I still did that sex and adultness didn't mix—adultness meaning intellect, fidelity, social value—I would have continued trying to reconcile them, but I would not, now, have been stuffing Margaret with my bulky ambition. I would, instead, have pursued the chance one has, at the age when one is apt to think in crude divisions, to divide myself among divided womanhood, attempting my reconciliation in alternating phases: sex with one woman, or a few, then a "relationship," then further experience of experiment. I would at last have admitted that I didn't know what I was doing, or that I knew what I was doing and didn't mind, because I was growing up, not grown up. I would have pursued the chance to exploit my high youth, which in my case had not been "wasted on the young" only because I hadn't used it. For all my lust for the brainy woman, I might as well have been born a "tit-man." My indoctrination in Ethical Cultural and medical professional values, the "wholesome," "constructive," "affirmative," "real" values of knowledge, conscience, service, had left me as undeveloped as any puerile nooky-chaser, and confused: lusting for the vagina behind the forehead.

Margaret at Clark, and I having missed the accident, I would have begun learning, at full sexual force, with a penis that had not aged a lifetime when I was just twenty, what my grim involvement with Margaret had prevented at eighteen, nineteen. I would have learned sex when nature is still offering sex as the overwhelmingly important thing to learn, and with a body easily overwhelmed by sex. (My failure with the Hyde Park prostitutes had been exceptional; usually I had been able to come with one rub against anything.) The space between sexual desire and sexual courage, which in high school had hurt as sharply as a stretched wound, and which, during the time of Margaret, had become infected with a frustrating version of satisfaction, would at last have healed.

I would have continued to learn, early, who was mine and who was not. I would have begun to learn, early, not to take what was there for the taking merely because it was there for the taking. I would have begun to learn, early, to look at—to consider—what I was being offered. I would have begun to learn, early, how not to cause pain. I would not have caused as much pain as I later did. The learning body would not have been its own injured interference.

Excluding the Hyde Park misadventure, in my sexual experience prior to the accident I had humped, through clothes, eight girls, exploratorily felt a few of these, merely kissed a few more. I had laid—my first lay—a New York prostitute who looked like a prison matron, delivered to me in a room in a whorehouse-hotel; Margaret; and the middle-aged prostitute in Paris. None of my sexual experience prior to the accident approached in disturbing gorgeousness the humping, feeling, or kissing. Nor had any since. Instead, at twenty-seven, the adolescent gap still irritated, and my nerves melted into confusion by the accident, I was sexually ill, as if involuntarily destructive. That winter, there were still other spasms in which I shook off women I grabbed to me.

I had been safely working, in the meantime, to make drama I could manage, telling a story of my life. Most of what I was making happen in the novel had not happened to me in fact; whatever in the novel had happened to me in fact was happening, in the novel, at different times, in different places, for other reasons, than it had happened in fact, to a streamlined and fantasized version of me, and in relation to characters composed of two or three actual people, or one quarter of an actual person, or all of fantasy, or of a mouth of fact in a face of fantasy. My novel was taking my accident and making it theoretical, putting it "on paper." I was mowing down the trees of my youth and turning the space into a plot, where events were visibly caused, connected, and resolved. In the novel, Eric Green had broken his neck as I imagined one should break one's neck—for the sake of literary sense, for the sake of relevant "punishment," the way Tolstoy's Ivan Ilyitch develops cancer. Eric Green had broken his neck falling down a flight of stairs while chasing his girlfriend, Hilary, who in fury had walked out of an argument concerning Eric's self-centeredness. He had been preparing for the leading role in the Warriner College production of *Richard II*—a projection of, among other things, the once projected *Hamlet*—and gotten so taken up in his role that Hilary's value to him had diminished dangerously. (Hilary was the costume designer for the show.) Rising, falling, arrogance, punishment; the replacement of a shame I had not fully acknowledged with a classic self-disgust I could manipulate. I was not learning or explaining myself, for "I" was not in the book, but, rather, providing a clear "reason" for an unreasonable event, giving accident thematic support, and its victim an ultimate victory—the loss of arrogance, the defeat of punishment. I knew the story as I did not know the story of my own life. The novel asked no questions. Yet it had philosophical urgency, a reason for being, beneath the artist's reasons. The reason was reason itself. Inventing, magnifying, shrinking my history into artistic convenience, I was not aiming, primarily, to disguise myself— has anyone who has *not* had a broken neck ever written a novel about someone with a broken neck?—but trying to write about the only event in my experience that wanted novelistic making up. A novel would make me new, news.

By April of 1961, I had finished what I felt to be the first half of my novel. I gave it, and an outline of the remainder, to Doubleday. In May, eight years to the month since the accident, and a few days before my twenty-eighth birthday, Doubleday bought the novel. I made dozens of phone calls of announcement to family and friends. I lay down on my bed to experience my success. I breathed the color—a Renaissance color, a violin's color—of the late afternoon spring light. I lay on my back, my relief lying on me. I felt an excitement of relaxation. I felt as if I had been put together again. I felt confirmed. In our correspondence over the winter, Doubleday, while encouraging me, while assuming my talent, had been concerned that my novel—as I had presented it to them in a general outline—might turn out to be "self-conscious," "introspective," "analytical" (in effect paralyzed, though I do not think they were thinking of this implication), to the cost of drama, action, and spontaneity. So, in buying the novel, for an amount of money that, though modest, was greater than the customary minimum for first novels, they had not, after all, bought me off; they had bought me in the faith that the second part of my novel would be as good as they had discovered the first to be. I had accomplished a monumental transaction—the selling of *my* talent for praise, faith, world-money. I had literally redeemed myself. I had made my disaster pay by shrewdly converting it to art, like someone smuggling himself out of tyranny. Living by my wits, I had outmaneuvered peril. Just because I would not likely have become a novelist in a parallel life did not mean it was easy to have become one now. And I was, now, already a novelist; I had been certified. I felt so much energy for completing the novel that it was as if the novel were completed. What could happen to it? If it was alive, it must be completely safe, as, after the accident, since I was alive, I would never die. Not only was it as good as finished, but, when published, it was going to sell seventy-five thousand copies. That many people would be unable to resist my tale of triumph, I decided, in my triumph. In the letter that accompanied the contracts, a few weeks after the sale, my editor, Ellin Roberts, called me "a very gifted writer," called herself "proud and grateful to be involved at the start of what I confidently hope will be a very successful literary career," looked forward to our lunch date two weeks hence, and admonished me to take my vitamins. I was prized, contracted for, to be lunched. I was necessary. I was made of value. I was a novelist. "Who's your publisher?" "Doubleday." "Oh!" Being a certified novelist is distinguished no matter how distinguished a novelist you are, and even if you haven't finished your novel. Acknowledging, however, that even with a contract one is a more distinguished novelist if one's novel is finished, and yet having to recognize that the novel was only half-finished, I arranged immediately to have my photograph taken for the book-jacket; then, to justify the photograph, to give it a place to be put, to cover the space between it and me, I hurried back to work.

In April, at a wedding (my third time as best man), I had met Rochelle, and she became, in May, an emblem of the merit I attained by selling my novel, a prize for my song. I had earned her, she was worth earning, appreciable, a reward for hope and a stimulus of hope. Rochelle was subduedly cheerful, shyly cordial, demurely earthy. She was funny in a sad voice. Her outlook was her own, and she was a graduate student, in a field arcane to me; she was, therefore, according to my crude respect for intelligence, a woman who "knew what she was doing," who could "take care of herself," a woman whom I cared to respect, and whom I couldn't damage if I wanted to. I took my time with her. I didn't want to pass through her, which meant that I didn't need to pass through her. On my bed with her, after a few meetings, I was timorous. I plucked inquiringly at her clothes until she murmured, "Here, let's get these off." Mature, womanly. Her body was solid. We enjoyed each other without desperation. A balm of loving passivity covered me. Our sex was as if silent; not grave—we smiled, we grew to make genital jokes—but gentle. I didn't, with Rochelle, feel I needed to come; we screwed calmly. Perhaps the sexual panic and hostility of the winter had shamed me into a probationary peacefulness; perhaps the sale of my novel allowed me to feel I had no need to sell myself; Rochelle was involved with a man to be published. If I had arrived, I did not have to come. I didn't feel myself to be in love with her, but I wasn't pretending to be; nor did I feel that I urgently needed her. Not hungry, I had appetite for her virtues. She was easy to appreciate.

None of her emotions stuck out sharply. She had no edges on which I could hurt myself. Everything was draped. But, over the summer, her subduedness itself seemed to thicken. And I didn't want to penetrate it. It said not to bother. Behind it I would find forlorn inaccessibility. When I'd had enough gray peace, Rochelle said I'd betrayed her—she'd been emerging, and now she'd have no one to come out to.

I'd seen thickening where she'd seen thinning. But I trusted myself. I had been right to be interested in her and right to lose interest. Rochelle did for me what she claimed I had stopped doing for her: she elicited my health. If some of luck is our sense that we're worthy of it, then Rochelle helped make me ready for Sarah.

TEN

As, under contractual blessing, I concentrated daily on creating the story of Eric Green's accident and recovery, as I used my brain in a way only I could, my brain gained size. A novel in the making is, to its author, literally as huge as an ocean, no matter how mere a glass of water it may be to a reader, no matter how mere a glass of water it may be. My novel was becoming a new ocean in the world, displacing land of fact. I was competently arranging and controlling the currents, temperatures, depths, winds, waves, colors, horizons, the consequences of this expanding reality. Brain-power. I could not, working on my novel, have been less oblivious, irresponsible, careless. I knew, I could remember, each inch of my ocean, where each inch of it was in relation to each other inch, and if I had to find something far back in the manuscript, I could find it instantly. It was like learning an enormous part for a play, like the twins' roles in *Ring Around the Moon*. If one didn't dominate, retain, one went under. I had the whole novel between my arms, beneath my eyes, in my head. I was gigantic. Meeting Rochelle, I'd been a newly licensed novelist; I'd enjoyed flashing the license. Meeting Sarah, I'd had enough months' further experience to grasp the size of what I was experiencing. The writing of the book had become more important than its publication. I didn't feel accomplished so much as that I was accomplishing something tremendous. I deserved Sarah's

splendid intelligence and her physical charm, and her significant vitality—the enthusiasm in her gestures, speech, and face,
her general confidence, anticipation, glee. And I deserved her
need for me.

She picked me out at the engagement party where we met.
We talked, throughout the evening, as if we were pounding a
shared drum. We agreed so ferociously that we might have been
arguing. We talked mostly about writers, writing, and, as with
Jill four years earlier, recent plays. Though in a way less sophisticated than Margaret (Margaret, with her cherished, though
often valuable, peculiarities of information, was more sophisticated than she was anything else), Sarah gave off a sense of
intellectual pleasure that made Margaret's brain frozen cauli-
flower by contrast. Less of an intellectual, as such, more secular,
than Lizzie, she seemed to me, if possible, intellectually even
sexier. Her words were kisses in my head. She was talking in
the ideal way for me.

Sarah knew with an ease that I envied and adored what,
though I knew it too, I was still discovering, as if I hadn't yet
seen quite enough documentation: that art was to be used,
that art was *functional* example, that Shakespeare was to be
quoted *behaviorally*, and not alone "as the poet says"; that we
must borrow from Cordelia and be warned by Lear, and reminded of ourselves by Ivan Ilyitch and Lolita and Humbert
Humbert and Captain Ahab and Moby Dick; that characters
from plays and paintings and cartoons, novels, operas, movies,
ballets, that lines of poems and measures of music, were part
of our lives as much as they were part of their own; that art
was analogy and analogy the chief way we understand anything
we have not understood before; that art was to be applied and
then incorporated; that art was the title of life: it stood for
and participated in. Though she was my age, and though she
was not a writer, or an artist of any kind, Sarah knew this as
if she had known it for years. Perhaps it was easier for her to
know because she was not an artist, or the child of scientists.

But most of what she knew most people didn't know. She was an extraordinary citizen, a citizen who thought. She understood, without cynicism or fuss, when a play or book was inflated or half-baked; she could quickly and precisely analyze the dough in the puff. She disliked with as much concern as I, but she was more efficient, less personally offended, in her disapproval, and less emotional than I in her approval. I composed my criticism from the ground up; she seemed, rather, to present hers, elegantly, directly, and in depth.

Much of what we exchanged that night, in public, in full voice, could not have been more intimate. The matters of art we discussed were crucial to us, someone else's radical politics. Few people are comfortable hearing another's views urgently expressed, especially if they involve nothing more than a play or a book. Sarah, this stranger who had emerged from time, this lovely, new, familiar woman, cared as much as I. We exchanged intensity.

On my way to the age of twenty, I had often felt suspect when fervent about a work of art, or even when excited by love. Not at home, usually, and not among my closest friends, usually, but in "the world." Classmates, I felt, were suspicious. "What's *he* so excited about?" I felt that my emotional displays made me odd and insincere, a performer out of place, as my father had charged me with being the night he'd attended the concert of the school chorus. I must have felt that the suspicion I could feel on me made some sense, because I knew how aware I was of my involvement, how conscious of my ecstasy, how proud to be weeping at an opera, or to be so moved at a play that I couldn't applaud, or to be laughing so hard at a Marx Brothers movie that I couldn't breathe. When thirteen or so, walking home alone from *A Song to Remember* (Cornel Wilde as Chopin), having just lost the virginity of my art-loving tears, I said to myself, "I cried, I am crying" (crying at having cried). At fifteen, I was so thrilled with my grief at *Death of a Salesman* that I saw the play twice. As a standee at *A Streetcar*

Named Desire, I slumped nearly to my ankles at the final curtain. And it was the grief-thrill, the slumping, that I would report first, then what it was that had so affected me. Yet after all, despite my self-consciousness, my sexual sort of bragging, my responses were out of my control. After all, the literary adolescent's lust for artistic suffering, routinely mocked as weltschmerz or affectation, is, in fact, honest and understanding, even if it may be innocent of its own implications, and too often open-armed. Tragedy is beautiful in art because the tragic victim's last-minute knowledge redeems the audience. Tragedy is hope.

By the time I met Sarah, I was comfortable observing my emotions, and announcing them. I understood now that self-consciousness and sincerity could coexist, as a comic, ironic human combination. I chose more carefully whom I bragged to. At the same time, it made less difference whom I bragged to, because everyone else was older and more comfortable along with me. But my responsiveness itself, for reasons both not uncommon and uncommon, had aged, too.

At the theater, in particular, I was less excitable. I squinted harder at plays. My judgment was shrewder, while the theater, all on its own, was shrinking. But I couldn't entirely trust my judgment. I knew that my momentous personal experience had helped to make me irritable with much theater. (I was going to too many plays, perhaps because I could, also because I continued to hope for kicks.) I could not tolerate, for instance, the wistful "absurdism" of *Waiting for Godot.* My still unfamiliar, and uncomfortable, sense of myself as a model survivor, who coped so well he didn't admit even having to cope, could easily reduce for me plays that for most others were "tremendous." So, I was older, smarter, more critical, "different," and the theater seemed younger (or had it remained the same?), frequently stupid, and less critical. I had company. My friends were beginning to outgrow most of serious Broadway and off-Broadway; most serious new theater now belonged to people who, row upon row, munched the hot clichés they were served and wiped their hands applauding. For my friends and me, the new was often tired. I might dismiss a whole play while friends found something good to say about it, I might be angrier or more disappointed than they, but I could not be called a crank. I wanted to love what I went to. For anything larger than I was I had no difficulty finding enthusiasm. I exhorted friends to go to what I loved. I could still drop tears at a moving stage-moment. I could laugh as hard as I had in the years before the accident.

But I laughed hard differently; I had trouble making laugh-noise. Because my chest muscles were weak, it was easier for me to laugh in than out. I wondered, with a stealth my anxiety insisted on, whether, even though the opinions of others assured me there was less to respond to, I didn't have less to respond with; whether the joy and grief the theater now found hard to come by, I didn't find equally hard to come by, as I did with women. I couldn't *feel* as much as I had felt before the accident, on my skin or on my heart's skin. I suspected myself of too little emotion, as I had suspected myself, in my earlier life, of too much. Evidence that there was less to respond to lost most of its importance if my emotions had atrophied, if my maturity was pathological. For all the experience, theatrical and human, that I insisted on; despite the excitement I had raised for Nicole and Deborah, and maintained for Lizzie and Jill, was I as if amputated without knowing it? Was I, beyond my control, out of touch?

In 1957, during the visiting Old Vic's production of *Romeo and Juliet,* when Tybalt stabbed Mercutio, and Romeo, terrified, said to his friend, "Courage, man. The hurt cannot be much," and Mercutio, dying, answered his old answer. "No, 'tis not so deep as a well, nor so wide as a church door; but 'tis enough, 'twill serve," I felt as if I had been punched from behind. My head slammed forward, and, though for no longer than it takes to exhale a breath, I sobbed. I had not known until that moment that I possessed any grief for myself. But my grief could produce no more liquid than it would, in two years, for my father. I think I grieved less for the depth or width of my pain than because my pain was not enough, it did not serve.

Talking with Sarah at the party where we met, I felt as I had in my room at Columbia, listening to *Great Festivities at the Capulets'*—physically overjoyed. I might have been doing a boiling dance. It was as if I'd predicted this night when I called my father, after hearing the music, to tell him how exciting it was going to be to live. My excitement seemed to congratulate me. It did not cause my love but came from it, and my love was admiration: for the thoughtfulness and independence of Sarah's talk. Admiration lets the admirer feel admirable. I had no sense, as perhaps I should have had, of being sexually distracted or impatient, no sense that I could possibly waste her. There seemed to be no need to be distracted; I was listening to sex. It was concentrated in Sarah's confident, trustworthy intelligence, in her verve, in our copulating unanimity. Or else I did not allow myself sexual underthoughts. Sarah was mine, nearly me, we were nearly one another, twins. But almost as much as we belonged to one another, or a bit more than we belonged to one another, we didn't. We were able to talk with luxurious intensity at luxurious length, our conversation coming to include some personal information, only because Sarah's husband had been leaving us alone all evening. I admired her so much, and so wanted to be appreciated by her, that, if necessary, I would leave her alone after the evening had ended. She was as forbidden as a Capulet, and I was unable to be, at first, greedy for her.

I could manage to leave her alone, but I resented her leaving me alone. I was relieved when she telephoned from her office one morning late in the autumn to say she'd like to have lunch with me. She had been absorbing me in the interim, she said, me and my accident. She came to my apartment for sandwiches. Her importance and her marriage kept me cautious. We had a "light" lunch for most of it, the best of friends, not lovers limp with sweated heat. But there we were, briskly and ebulliently continuing to narrate our lives, not at all the best of friends, not reclining against familiarity, not exchanging gossip or telling jokes. Alone with each other, we were in danger. By the end of lunch, we were slipping our hands beneath our words, which dancingly meshed between us, joining and separating us. Our hands touched conversationally while testing for shocks. When she left, we kissed on the mouth, hurriedly.

I received from her a bewildered letter. Who was I? Where had I come from, to distract her so violently that all of her life but me had become a distraction? (She did not ask why I had come; if she felt anger or sorrow, she did not know it or show it. But she was upset, in the most literal way. Her life's shape had been changed. Why do we make an enormous amount of room for a stranger where there had seemed to be no room? Love is a bully.) I must have been intimidated by her awed puzzlement, by the power of mystery she gave me. I answered her "Who are you?" facetiously, by listing people I was and wasn't. I might deserve Sarah, but could I bear deserving her? If I couldn't bear deserving her, did I deserve her? Could I carry the weight of her value? If not, then how could I possibly carry the weight of her value plus the weight of her marriage? In my facetious reply to Sarah, I dropped love on her toes. As strong as I felt now, now I couldn't believe my own strength. Love is a bully all around. I could infer what was wrong, theoretically, with her marriage by the glee with which she talked with me. But maybe there was nothing wrong with her marriage but her; or maybe she liked her marriage, and wanted me along with it. During her marriage's modest length had she been struck by anyone before me? It did not seem possible, but it was possible: did she make a practice of me? The blessing of her great interest, while it heated up my confidence, melted parts of it. In effect, I asked the question people often ask when they have been selected by disaster: why me? I had never asked it about the automobile accident. The accident of Sarah made me ask.

I did not know how much of her I could take. I did not know how much of me she wanted. I was so agitated by my own ignorance, it didn't occur to me that she herself likely didn't know. Even though, or because, I had already invaded her, I felt I could be an imposition, and that she would have to turn me away when I said that I wanted to see her again. What right did I have? Had she given me the right? What right did she have? Did she and her husband go their "separate ways"? Did he know about me and not care? Did he know about me and not care because he supposed I couldn't be a sexual threat? It might be that I was being asked by Sarah deeper backstage than I had ever gone. But I did not know. I did not know whether I was being asked. I did not know whether I should go if I was being asked. I telephoned Sarah at her office. I took an imperative step of pursuit. The floor squealing, silent voices shushing me, I said to her, let's do something together again, lunch, a museum, a movie, whatever. Fine, she said; let's.

We accumulated meetings, lunch, drinks after work, evening, her work her excuse, or her husband out of town. No children tugged her home. We met at my house, at an unpopular restaurant, an unlikely bar, and we talked, we talked, we talked. Sarah talked, now, more than I, more and more, it seemed to me. But my seizure of dismay that I might have fallen in with a predatory gabber, that she talked not out of need to talk to me in particular but because she couldn't help herself once she found a pair of available ears, dissolved and spread in warm particles of anticipation. Sarah's volubility, I realized, had multiplied for the same reason that mine had thinned. Sarah might talk and talk, yet the strength of her intelligence had not been used up by our second, third, sixth meeting. She had intellectual health to spare because her surroundings (I was now among them) fascinated and invigorated her. The force of her informed intensity endured. The longer I knew that her brain was what I had loved it for being at first, the more I thought about her body, our bodies. I had become impatient, distracted. Her electricity had entered my ears to shoot about my nerves like light. She talked to postpone the silent sexual conversation our vocal brain-kissing had made inevitable. She had become more apprehensive than I, and, I could see, she had more reason. My sympathy for her very nervousness, my gratitude for it, helped me to trust her.

It was my turn to move us. She had brought us so far; she waited for my help. I would have to be cautious now not for the sake of safety but for the sake of success. I would have to be cautious dynamically, responsible actively. I could no longer do my part by leaving her alone. Sarah was the first person I had ever known, other than myself, whom I'd consciously wanted to take in hand in order to protect, and whom I felt to be mine to influence—she was married, but she didn't have parents at her shoulder—and worth influencing. Because she was so enormously considerable, and because she was married, I wanted to, while I had to, consider her. She was the first woman in either life to give me power I could see and hold. Also, though married, Sarah was future. I was courting her. While I declared myself, showed my honorable intentions of desire, I would have to make it as comfortable as it was imperative for her to accept me. I would have to show my urgency or I would be failing her. I had to insist on her. But insistence was dangerous. Her love, in the way I held it, might seem to her too important to me. She could take her importance away from me. Or she could return to me my importance. Or she might not trust my urgency: my love might appear unreal to her, or unrealistic, impetuous, selfish. My love, as it turned out, let me be careful in my courtship without being strategic, insistent without storminess. My love, or our love, or love, made me graceful. It was as if what love required love performed. It seemed to take over, to have come to serve us.

We kept sexually aloof. There was no further touching of hands—verification of heat. We kissed only to kiss quickly good-bye, someone else's wife and her good friend. Nor did we talk much about sex. Sex had become the subject, and so was not among the subjects we discussed. We talked as if we knew that having brought each other up to date on our separate histories, and kept each other up to date on our separate presents, we would move into a future we shared. We were waiting for our future to make up the bed. Caution, fear, assurance, allowed me an uncharacteristic implicitness (Sarah's, like most women's, was characteristic). The little we spelled out we spelled out rarely, and almost never fully. I told Sarah, well on in our talk-ing, that I was sexually unreliable, and that I hadn't come in the eight years since the accident. She said, as if she were a doctor who had reason to know (and I recall that during this conversation I was lying on my bed and she was sitting in a chair nearby), that she was sure it didn't have to be that way. I asked her about herself. She felt herself to be very responsive, she said; sensitive. Though by this time I had certainly made it clear that I wanted, more than any other thing there was in the world to want, to go to bed with her, Sarah had not made it clear that she was going to go to bed with me; but our exchange meant that I was warning her how I was going to be in bed with her; and that she, for her part, was going to be trying to prove to me that I could come after all; and that I would be learning firsthand how sensitive she was.

Implicitness could carry us just so far. We had to move—two of us had to move—from chairs to bed. Early in the winter, I wrote Sarah a sonnet—a silent speech but an act of literary gallantry, meant to be decisive—formally urging her to "accept my love." She read the sonnet and told me she would not see me for a week, while she thought. More often than not, when people are "going to think," they have already thought, and de-cided "no," and are stalling. But I knew, as if I had skipped pages, that the next time Sarah and I were together we would begin to give up our bodies, turn them over to each other. I knew, too, that she had skipped the same pages. In her week alone, she would be accustoming herself, from its threshold, to the light of a cave that had risen unexpectedly from the ground of her life. When, in a week, she called to say she was coming to see me as early as possible later that afternoon, I didn't ask, "Have you decided?" or "What have you decided?" I knew; and I wouldn't have dared. I felt as if, were I to ask, I might be proved wrong, or that asking might prove me wrong, that silence itself would surely keep me right. Silence was darkness. We needed darkness. And silence was unforced growth. As much as I wanted to control what happened to us, what I wanted to happen would happen only if I kept my hands at my sides. We were growing together. Only unforced growth would join us accurately, generatively. I waited for Sarah in the cave.

During the courtship, we had been too old to provoke each other sexually unless we were going to screw, and too scared to provoke each other to screwing. Now we lay like the kinds of adolescents we had been ten years before, fully clothed, kissing in tense tenderness, then looking at one another's eyes to make sure we were there. A day or so later, we tried some touching. A day or so after that, we took off our clothes. Sarah's underpants were pink. She knew, from our months of personal anecdote, that I hated pink underwear. I laughed hard to see her pants, she laughed hard at my laughing. Our laughter was victorious. Each time I added Sarah up, her sum increased. It overjoyed me that amidst our sobriety, our fear, she could make a joke for us, that she could dare to, and be so right to have done so. I suppose it reminded her, and me, that our arrival at sex was not the carrying out of a suicide pact; that, though we were taking a dangerous dive, and taking it for her husband, too; though we were breaking law and wrenching marriage, we were also simply taking our clothes off to love each other with our bodies. Though sex changed lives, it was also only sex. Though sex was a Wagnerian poison, it was also charming, silly. Sarah had hung a touch of lightness in our solemn hiding place.

With the removal of her underpants, I was sliding almost immediately down the flour-fine beach of her flesh, skin that felt more like skin than any skin I had ever felt, skin peculiarly mine, skin I could not quite believe to be mine. I was, at last, just past twenty, without the accident having happened. I pushed backward, through the mild defense of her hand (as if at the risk of popping a dream), and continued on my coastal glide. I did not want my penis tested, though it was bulging, brushing her as I slid. (She was feeling it along her thigh and leg, she feeling my penis.) More than I did not want my penis tested—that, most of all, could pop the dream—I wanted to see secrecy, greet it. If I could not see Sarah's brain, I could see the secret of her body. And I wanted, above all, to love her in the most personal possible way, to excite the secret more personally than a penis can, or than my penis could. I used my fear to my advantage. I made her glad she hadn't stopped me. In our cave, I kissed her cave. Her cave had never been kissed. It had been entered, but never seen.

I wrote to her once:

It is poignant to me to love so especially in one what everyone has. Is it a way to general knowledge, to love someone really? The entire world rushes into you, you contain it, and yet it contains you. You could not be more individual. You are individual because you have what everyone has but it belongs to you, and in no one else would I find the sense of universality. It is you who is universal, only you. . . . It is so clearly, helplessly human for nipples to harden and spring out. But that they are yours doing it drives me wild with appreciation for your appreciation. *You* responding universally to *me*. Anyone else's response would be merely particular, and boring. . . . Just to put a hand on your belly makes enough quiet noise in me to last a day—a thud, like a softly stroked bass drum, of complete contentment, but it is not such a sexual moment as a warm one, possessive, easy, friendly. It is like a field of calm surrounded by volatile places. Your hips jump, they are electric, they are shockable, and they shock me at the moment I shock them. Your thighs I love because they're solid, and healthy, and well-shaped, and for what they lead to. I love them for supporting you, and for what's between them. And as for that, all I can say of it is that, like you, it's the only one in the world.

Into this hole meant for me my penis would glide. Wet electricity. Sarah would squint as she slid slowly up and down me, concentrating so hard she looked old. She whimpered when she came, thrilling me. She always came, and she came for both of us. If my penis shriveled inside her or did not fatten outside her, I kissed her to coming, burrowing, unable to get enough of her vaginal opulence, smearing my nose, mouth, and chin. She showed impatience only with my pressing her for patience. When anxious, I would try to make her admit she was a sexual materialist, in effect. I could not always quite believe that she was getting what she wanted (that, indeed, she had stopped having sex with her husband), and that I was that thing. I became other than what she wanted not by not coming, much as she wanted me to come, but by supposing that in not coming I was letting her down. I let her down when I supposed I was letting her down. If I thought myself a failure, then she would have to think herself a failure. She refused me weakness. I kept having to give up to her love.

I was hers. When she left for the afternoon or evening, I delayed washing her off me for as long as I could. Strokes of recollection made me wince, slump, and dwell, as if I were heartbroken. She seemed to have peeled away all my numbness. She surrounded me. She left herself in my sheets. (Often I added to her by sleeping with a pair of her underpants by my nose.) She filled my apartment. She filled the air, the light, wherever

I went. I talked to her when I was talking to others, and when others were talking to me she was commenting from inside my head. She defined me.

At a certain heat, intensity cracks into paradox. As much as Sarah was reality, she was magic; loving her brought my ear to the heart of music, where the pain is the cure.

That winter, I went, with my family, to Zeffirelli's production of *Romeo and Juliet*. I wept there as I had never wept, in a theater or out, in either life. Through the party scene at the Capulets', the lovers, having discovered each other, moving slowly, in awe, down the opposite sides of a triangle of oblivious guests, meeting at the apex to flirt gravely with one another's adoration; and through the complete confessions of the balcony scene, I cried, grinning, a wet mess, in love with Juliet and Romeo, in love with Sarah, in love with me, in love with Sarah and me, my tears coming as easily as looking. They arrived at my eyes and gently leaped, by the hundreds, as if they had been occupying me and now they were liberating me. Each time I wiped my eyes, a fresh batch tumbled out, until I was light and sore with relief.

In late October, I had turned in the completed first draft of my novel to my former employer. After a few weeks, I got from Ellin Roberts a general sort of letter, praising my writing as such, and certain characters and scenes, pointing out some weak areas, and warning me I had work to do. While she was on vacation, she would have the manuscript read by another senior editor and the Editor-in-Chief.

In December, after these readings, and some rereading by her, my embarrassing concern that Doubleday, in buying my book, had tried to soothe me with an attractive form of severance pay, received a solid and final kick. An eight-page, single-spaced letter from Ellin—an essay on my novel—consolidating her profoundly thorough criticisms with those of her two colleagues, plus three pages of notes referring to technical, literary, and substantive problems throughout the text, made it impossible for me to doubt that Doubleday was taking my book seriously; if anything, more seriously than I; in fact, seriously to the point that Ellin wrote: "And, as I'm sure you don't need to be told, our sole combined concern is that this first novel of yours will be just as good as it possibly can, so that it will redound to your credit and, we can hope, to your profit. The fact that our credit and profit are intimately joined to yours hardly figures . . . for the simple and obvious reason that Doubleday has lots of eggs in its basket, whereas at the moment you have just this one in yours." If the letter had cheered my book on as potentially lucrative, I would have suspected Doubleday of continuing condescension.

Arriving at the editors' essential criticism, Ellin wrote, ". . . at some point Eric must really just about break down. He must be truly hurt . . . he hasn't been, despite the accident. His tears when they occur are good, but there is a restraint in your handling of him that keeps the book from achieving a moment of real emotional power and urgency. . . . To make his injury, his pain, shame, humiliation, and frustration meaningful to readers who have not had his exact experience, I think you've got to bring him, and thus his audience, to some kind of fresh awareness or conclusion. . . ."

I understood that Eric must be truly hurt. If Eric wasn't hurt enough, the reader wouldn't hurt enough. But, though I didn't know it, I didn't want Eric to be hurt enough. And my brazen objectivity—the public distance I had arranged between me and my injury, shame, humiliation, and frustration by writing the novel in the first place, and by writing it, full of literary virtue, with fierce attention to its superstructure, substructure, and style —had succeeded in keeping my suffering, in Eric's possession, smaller than life-size. The fact is that, while I yearned for pain, I had not yet earned the separation from my own injury, shame, humiliation, and frustration that would allow me to recognize them openly, no less show them to others, even in a novel about "someone else." It would be injurious, shameful, and humiliating to recognize them. As I revised the manuscript through the early months of 1962, and Sarah was tenderly restringing my nerves, I strained to loosen my careful style so that I might pass some pain through it to Eric. But I was still too young, my fingers were too weak, to help him to much pain. I was only old and strong—and lucky—enough to be helping myself to Sarah.

Normally we did not see each other on weekends, like adulterers the world over, and during many weekends we were unable to speak on the phone. We had each other to think about and to look forward to, and we saved up everything to tell. We saved up everything to tell, but now we did more of our talking on the phone than we did face to face. It had become nearly impossible for us to be in my apartment and talk at length before we had fed on flesh.

However busy I might be when I wasn't with Sarah, I thought about her on the average of every other pulse beat. One of the things about her I thought most, on weekends, was, would she be able to come on Monday? If she were unable to come on Monday, something might develop on Monday that would prevent her from coming on Tuesday, or she might get the flu on Monday and be unable to come to me for a week or weeks. It was as if, were I not to see her when I was next supposed to see her, I might never see her again. It was as if each of her arrivals meant the saving of the world, each postponement a distinct encouragement to death. Once, when she phoned to say she wasn't going to be able to make it that day, I threw a glass against the wall.

In his "Reflections on Gandhi," George Orwell concludes: "The essence of being human is . . . that one is prepared in the end to be defeated and broken up by life, which is the inevitable price of fastening one's love upon other human individuals." So prepared, though, one is all the more unprepared. The sense of cruciality that a love like Sarah's and mine can bring on makes the possibility of defeat by life intolerable. The end of such critical, such dependent, love hid, for me, in every setback life provided. I felt our love, for all its vastness, to be perilously exposed to circumstance. Whatever happened to Sarah happened to me. Trusting her so heavily, I could not trust circumstance to support my trust.

On a weekend in May, separated from her, I leaked tears. I thinned and softened, as if my lungs had become my skin. I felt as if I were being nauseated by a grief composed of desire and gratitude. I didn't have to breathe to breathe, and my breaths were huge, opening great space in me I had not owned before. I felt as if I were dying outward, weakening into nature, poisoned by tenderness.

On the Monday ending that weekend, I came, in Sarah's mouth, sudden, unpreventable rivers rising over my hips, late for the ocean, flooding the rear of my penis, and in their confluence blasting through me at three times my thickness, alarming me. My legs went berserk, bucking like violent flames. Sarah swallowed, making startled, gulping, loving noises. She looked at me, then, smiling. As offhandedly as she could, she congratulated me. I slammed my fist, once, into the pillow; my dream had come true.

After winning a critical game, an athlete may pound the bench before jumping up and down and pounding teammates; or one may slam a desk after receiving a phone call or opening a letter of critical good news. One has nailed something crucial and difficult, so one pounds in the nail, as if to secure success, or kill the defeated possibility of defeat, or kill resented tension, apprehension, one needed for the victory. But victors who pound the bench, the desk—or the bed—appear to be angry, as well, at victory. I know, now, that rushing into my fist, along with my vengeance on the outwitted jailer in my nerves ("I had it coming to me"), was a punch at my release. Who deserved such a "miracle"? Nine years! Found innocent! I had become accustomed to the silence of my penis, its perhaps appealing stoic inarticulateness. The point had been to be able to "do it," not to come, and I had learned to do it, to partner women with a mysterious, self-effacing kind of generosity. Now that I had come, I would have to come again. I would, furthermore, have to learn to come in the "right" place. My standard of expectation had leaped ten feet in an instant, after nine years of manageable rising. How could I make it? When I knew I was going to have to? I couldn't stand upright on my own. How could I jump? How was it that someone who couldn't walk could come? I suddenly didn't go with myself. As if I had been exploded, refractured, rearranged by an earthquake, I didn't match. I did not want to change again, enter a third life, or be returned, further than I had already been, to my first self. So, in my success, amazement, pride, and vengeance, I was frightend, if only for that immediate, seizing instant.

Thus, were I now able to walk again, to walk again would not be simple good fortune. I imagine I would be exposed, or feel exposed, in new dimensions, and to chilling dangers from reopened angles. I would be more susceptible to injury, and to injuring myself. I would have to handle all the shocked people, people too glad now rather than too sad, and a new self-consciousness. I would have to learn a kind of luck as unknown to us as moon-flight once was. But if my nerves could be rejoined fully, if I were told that the necessary surgery had been developed, I would have the surgery. I would have to make the choice to have more choices, to live higher and lower in the air, to hurry up and down steps, more steps, steps to more places, walk-ups, balconies, basement theaters, steppy stadiums, or to flow on escalators, to attend more special events, farewell recitals, rare performances, to which I would have expanded choice of access, seats well off the aisle, standing room. I would shop more often for small things. I would travel more often in ships and planes, be able to stay on the second floor of an inn in the British countryside, as I did when I was nineteen. I have not forgotten doing better what one can do better, more variously, more of, by standing, walking, running, crouching, jumping. I would play tennis, baseball, basketball, touch football, returning, like some of my friends, to the athleticism I outgrew in mid-adolescence to become a city boy. As much as I would grieve for the person I'd left behind, and worry my luck, and be angry that most of my life had passed—while now I am not angry that I do not walk—I would get used to walking.

The best of it would be the leisurely use of leisure, strolling, strolling to a movie, strolling in the country, lying down on grass and getting up from grass casually, on my own; meandering, conforming without thought to the contours of the natural world, its slopes, holes, mounds. When I went to the beach, I would swim in the ocean. It is difficult for me to take a vacation.

Growing up the first time, I had seen nature as stage sets for a dream theater, and declined responsibility for learning the details of my mother's garden, the birds my parents "watched," to identify like airplane spotters, and my father's scientific world, while I loved effects of light the stage could not achieve and colors that meant the general aesthetic drama of radiance, contrast, glamorous comfort: yellow, blue, white, blood-red, rose, greenness. Through my youth, I walked to school beneath immense trees; the road was a stage I had to myself. A meadow, a chartreuse lawn, woods, mountains, an ocean, were theater, as settings or as places containing potential surprise. I loved, I love, the ocean because there are things hidden in it; I have never been nearly so interested in those things as I am that they are there.

I absorbed atmospheres, auras. Inhaling the bathed nakedness of flowers, I dreamed of sex before I had heard of it. I played baseball on a wide, dusty field in a yellow twilight that put time to sleep, a scene of prolonged privilege in which I figured cozily. I biked down hills between high walls of leaves, spring air rushing into my throat like flute music. Such sensations were memory even while I lived them. I preserved them as they occurred; they had preserved themselves for me to preserve. During my youth, I felt the earth to be as opulent and vivid as it had been at its earliest. I lived in the clean beginning. The Hudson River emerged from myth with a tremendous muscular glitter. The sun in the early morning placed an orange gleam—always like the appearance of the world's first light— on my bedroom wall, and on my way downstairs I breathed in the profound titillation of orange juice—the color and the odor, for me, of encouragement and friendly mystery.

Now nature exposes me. I sit alone on the Lowenthals' lawn in Connecticut, in a ripe June twilight, basking, gazing, one of the things people do in the country, so I am for the time being comfortable; my passivity is appropriate. I stare out on an immense open stage of contented pastoral distance, thinking how the sun-fogged terrain resembles one of the late afternoon scenes from my childhood summers at my grandparents' house (southward of my friends' house, though I do not think this; my geographical awareness, never well developed, now retracts as soon as I leave my city routes, since I have subsided into being driven everywhere I go). The caretaker ambles over to me and remarks what a shame it is that I can't walk around, enjoy the countryside. I ignore him, while with my next breath my blood turns gray.

I visit Paul and Annette in upstate New York. With my arms wrapped around supporting shoulders, I stagger some yards to the pond in the field of their lawn. I am lowered into the water. A canvas lawn chair is tucked under me. I lean back. I sit in the water up to my neck, as if I were sitting on land, pleased, soothed, as close as I can come to immersion, conformance. I sit there for an hour. Such water-pleasure is hard to come by.

I visit Boris and Lynn on Fire Island. They have an ocean-front house. A wooden stairway of extreme steepness takes you to the beach. I had been down steps like these on my own, lain on the beach on my own, when I was eighteen, and later, after twenty, once been carried down and up, the steps being separately too high, and the staircase too steep and uncertainly banistered, for me to walk them. Often I have sat above the steps, in my wheelchair, getting the sun and the wind full force, and taking in the full sweep of the ocean, from a box seat, in effect. I have made do. But the toilet in this house is too low, and the bed is low enough so that I must be careful pushing up off it into my chair; my buttocks just make it to the very edge of the chair, and I "sit" for a second, waiting to learn whether I am sufficiently seated to push myself backward, or whether, moving an arm or a leg in order to get myself into pushing position, I will slip off the chair, to hang over the floor, as though I had a choice to make, before letting myself down to it, and calling for the help I'll need to get up.

I have had no trouble getting out to the Island, by car and the ferry (and have often made the trip, by taxi and ferry, myself); there is so much of the usual I can do. Today, though, looking out on the beach and ocean below me, I watch a child running a dog, men and boys throwing a ball, and I am brought up short. So much of the usual I cannot do. I am not separated, but I am not there. I can get there, but not there.

When I came into Sarah, I reached the true end of my physical return. Within a few days, I would combine coming with fucking, retrieve that classic combination for the first time since Margaret. There was, suddenly again, after nine years, plenty more wherever it came from. Having done it again, I would batter Sarah's diaphragm with my sperm over and over, over and over. Still, once I'd come that first day, there was, in one crucial sense, nothing more to do. I had got there but could go no farther, could only repeat, at another entrance, my arrival. And it was as if I recognized my new and final limits at the moment I escaped my last old limits. There would now be no more progress.

ELEVEN

THE NEW ORGASMS, as orgasms will, exhilarated my cells and left my bones feeling steam-bathed. They excited Sarah because all my responsiveness excited her, and this was more of it. But I had already shared with her what still felt like definitive joy and comfort. The comeless pleasure I'd taken from the very presence of her body in bed should, in fact, have demonstrated to me what she'd meant when reassuring me that she had what she wanted: our *love* was thrilling; in relation to the excitement of our coziness, coming was not that important, though it was our love that made my coming necessary, possible (and though if she'd been unable to come because I wasn't coming, for how long would we both have believed her?). While Sarah had made me ambitious, Sarah herself satisfied me. What my coming added to sex—sometimes subtracted from it—was not as much sexual as personal in a way distinct from sex, distinct, even, from Sarah.

That these revived orgasms were exciting to have, felt good, and excited Sarah could not be as important to me as the fact of their presence. My coming meant desire, trust, the luxury of appropriate dependence. My coming was tribute to Sarah. (I remained as unable to masturbate now as I'd been at any time since the accident.) Sarah, no one else, had arrived out of time to make coming necessary and possible. Still, for me to have come again signified, above everything else, neural health, an unexpected change for the better in my neural health. I could not bear to imagine losing the conventional knack of coming again exactly as I could not bear to imagine losing any other physical strength I had recaptured in my nine new years. What I had, I had to keep. If my nerves' connections were to loosen, I could slip all the way back to the road. So, now, at those times when I didn't come, hypochondriacally I searched for reasons. Too tired? Wrong angle? Too fast, too slow? Why had I succeeded last week, when I'd been exhausted? When I again came again, why did I? Superstitiousness was out of character for me. Prophecy—as in ESP or astrology—offended me. But I found myself, on occasion, interpreting my coming or failure to come as the announcement or silence of good luck. I played in a monthly Friday night poker game. If I was with Sarah on a poker Friday, sometimes when I was inside her, stretched stiff to the limit, trembling, straining to catch, I would think: if I come today, I will win tonight. If I don't, I will lose. I had located the sexual materialist.

No one knows where anyone has come from. My colleagues at the poker table did not know what I had been doing for an hour or so that afternoon. Brickner had a woman, but they did not know it—a permanent, beloved woman, married to someone. One of them could have been her husband. I was holding secret a woman with whom I had exchanged half my cells. Having finally found what those who cared most about me wanted for me most, I could tell only a very few of them that I had found it, and those few only with the most severe admonitions to guard the information. News that squirmed to be enjoyed was whispered and locked up.

I could not, in general, easily be known as I wished to be known. I had become, in my new life, an object of snap judgments, assumptions, presumptions, projections, expressed through glances, actions, words, and omitted words. People found it difficult to ask me questions about me. I had established in others, through my extra kind of differentness, extra interest, ignorance, hypothesizing, fear, anxiety, concern, identification, pity, sorrow, sympathy, friendliness. I could be regarded as the victim of a tragedy. I could be, in my wheelchair, an abstraction. I could easily be misrepresented. I could be overknown without being known at all. Thus women on the street marking me with the baby-loving smile, a dinner-party hostess serving my meat cut up for me, the grocery, once, sending my corn shucked. Friends, friends who love me, *contemporaries*, messing my hair, running a finger under my chin, pinching my cheek. These things are true. I do not make them up; though sometimes I make up what has not happened. Early in the new life, in a restaurant, the first time I'd ever had lobster in a restaurant, I was upset when the waiter tied a lobster bib around me, imagining he'd singled me out as too clumsy to keep myself clean, until someone explained to me that lobster bibs were standard for people ordering lobster. However, as I entered a restaurant once, a priest paused on his way past me to grasp my shoulders and bestow on me a long benevolent look. I stared back, too startled, too angry, to be angry. Drunks in bars or restaurants sometimes stand over me swaying, mumbling encouragement, sorrow, apt to think I am a wounded vet. An alcoholic woman who lives in my building—if we pass in the lobby or on the street when she is drunk—seizes me to kiss me. I must fling her arms off me. I have developed an extended peripheral vision and quick reflexes. I have learned to anticipate, to duck, to swat. A friend, drunk, came up behind me in a restaurant and jammed his tongue into my ear. I slammed my plate of apple pie against his crotch.

I watch myself, too. In certain circumstances, with certain people, I watch what I say, don't say. I protect myself against judgments, actual, potential, or imagined by me, that I am less able than I am in fact to engage, negotiate, participate, or detach myself, objectify, be realistic; against the assumption that —my circumstances so distorting—*I* am unable to see who I am, and others are. At Columbia, I was discussing *Lady Chatterley's Lover* with a good friend. Even though I trusted him—he treated me directly, lovingly, and without undue attention—I worried that he would think I scorned the book because he supposed I had to separate myself from Lord Chatterley's ignominy. I was at the time, like Chatterley, impotent. My friend didn't know this. And I didn't tell him. But my concern was not to protect a secret. At least half to the contrary, I wanted to protect my critical independence, my right to dislike the novel even though, like Chatterley, I was in a wheelchair and—for all I knew my friend imagined—impotent. I knew my friend well enough to say to him, in effect, look, you understand, don't you, that it's hard for me to say I dislike this book without supposing that others think I'm being solipsistic? This is a bad book whether or not I, like Chatterley, am crippled. He agreed, adding that he hadn't made the connection I had taken pains to sever. If my friend had been less intelligent, or intelligently loving (or hadn't disliked the book fully as much as I), he might have found it convenient to decide that my opinion of it—all the more so because of the defense I gave it—was suspect. I could have dinner with a one-time high school friend, who had become a political aide of White House rank, a man of undoubtable intelligence as defined by skillful, vigorous use of brain-power, and remind him of a moment years before when he'd slipped his hands into the skirt pockets of a schoolmate; and he could say to me sadly, "Oh, you live in the past," not understanding that the artist type retained tiny details, gestures, looks; and I, not having an answer ready for such an unexpected and such a solemn charge, or not wanting to appear defensive, or not wanting to argue with someone I hadn't seen for so long, sidestepped to a new subject. Perhaps he, associated now with prominence, power, with men who governed, did not want to be returned to his own past.

Exposed, in my ambiguous new existence, to the threat of assumptions, I became careful to whom I mentioned that I had seen such and such a television show (people having said to me, "You must spend a lot of time at home" or "I guess you don't get out much"), and careful to mention that I had been to such and such a party, movie, play, opera, concert (defending my physical repution—flexibility, endurance—as if I were running for office). I have learned that when I express my lack of interest in ballet, or my love for watching sports, people may attribute poignancy to me, or, in the case of ballet, judgment controlled by my physical circumstances; that they may not grant me objective judgment or taste, or my conventional share of subjectivity. Reading that William F. Buckley had never been to the U.N., in his twenty years in New York, before he became a delegate, stirred me up. I have never been to the U.N. I have no interest in visiting the U.N. But no one would have said to Buckley, "Well, it's harder for you." I go almost everywhere I want to go, almost as much as I want to, sometimes more. I am proud, too proud, of my busyness. I come across people who worry, aloud, that I am not busy enough, as if I could not be, as if—I imagine them imagining—I had a few volunteer friends who invited me places or took me "on an outing" from time to time. If I try to disprove such a challenge on the spot, I am still likely to sound ruffled, "defensive"; if, "maturely," I decline the challenge with silence, I may remain what the challenger has needed me to be—categorizable: at the edge of social activity, where, in fact, the challenger may be, where I am not. I am judged, far more than I live, in terms of incapacity. I am, sometimes, a dream others are having about themselves. Because of my obvious unusualness, strangers, acquaintances, friends when anxious, transpose what is ordinary for me, easy for me, into difficulty, achievement. One of the ways I am minimized is to be commended for nothing. I would like to be able not to care, ever, what others imagine, fail to imagine, about me. I would like to be able to let my life speak for itself. "I want to be liked for myself!" cries the cliché cripple (or millionaire or beautiful woman—anyone extraordinary). The crippledness is part of the self. Only a part. But my life doesn't speak easily for itself.

I am at a party. A stranger sits down beside me. He is twice my age. Like the five-year-olds who ask me, "How did you get in that thing, anyway?" or "Hey, can you walk?"—questions I answer, when asked by children, with ease, and gently—the man asks me, "How did you get here?" I am instantly infected by his problem. To have to answer the question irritates me. (I will have to answer it.) For one thing, the question sounds, in an undertone, like "Why are you here?" For another thing, it makes much of the independent taxi-travel I am able to take for granted. As soon as the question is asked, *I* am the child. As if I must account. As if I am too young to travel about the city at night on my own. If I answer, "By ambulance," either the man will believe me or I will hurt his feelings with facetiousness. I cannot suppose, at the moment, that one who asks such a question possesses a playful spirit. If I wheel away from him without answering, I will seem to make too much of my own feelings, will be too hurt, bruise the atmosphere. So, I serve his need. "By taxi," I say. Then, trying to get something back for myself, I explain, "It happens to be easy for me. There's nothing to it." Only if I put him at ease, or imagine I put him at ease, can I put myself at ease. Then I can take myself away from him.

Another party. An outstanding, a famous, actress, whom I admire—I particularly don't want to be minimized by her—asks me, her gin sloshing over her dress, "How did you get this way?" "Syphilis," I say, hoping to lighten her attitude. But she is too drunk to be anything but sober about me. She insists, her eyes lugubrious. Please tell me. "Syphilis! Syphilis!" I say, smiling hard. But she won't be deflected. I have to go away from her. If I tell her the simple truth, she will grab me, or weep.

One does not ask people, Why are you fat, skinny? Why is your skin so pocked? Why do you have nine fingers? How did your stuttering start? Why is your nose so big? I am a public secret. I demand curiosity. I am, just being there, provocative. Sticking way out, helplessly I poke attention. The anxious poke back. Not often, but any time. They poke back, or grab hold.

Another party. Much drinking. I need the bathroom. I cannot get my chair through the bathroom door. I cram myself into a corner by the bathroom, and urinate into my bottle, the bottle's traveling cloth covering me. A woman I do not know approaches me from the side. "Excuse me," I say. "I'm busy here." She stays, watching me. "Excuse me," I say again. "I need to be left alone." She doesn't move, says nothing. I turn as far from her view as I can, finish, zip myself up. When I leave the party, the woman and her husband are in the elevator with me. They ask me where I live. "It's O.K.," I say. "How will you get home?" "It's fine," I say. "By cab. Do it all the time. Nothing to it." They say, "We'll help you." I say, "No, please, don't bother." We're on the street. I hail a cab. The couple watch me get into the cab, watch the cab-driver fold the chair, put it in the cab. The couple follow me into the cab. I cannot shut the door in their faces, or say, "Leave" or "Leave me alone." There is something wrong with them, but not with me. After all, I am not a woman being pursued by a physically threatening man, or about to be held up. We ride across town, three abreast, barely talking. My bladder is still drinking. I must urinate again. I explain this to the couple. "It's all right," they say. "We understand." In the cab, beside them, I urinate. When I get home, my good-bye is sullen. Sarah arrives. Gulping, my voice shaking, I tell her the story.

I am only *more* overknown and misknown than others. Others, too, are appropriated, misrepresented, or secrets. None of us can always know the whole story of what has happened, or where someone is going, or know what is happening in front of us, no less behind us, or backstage of anything. People pass secrets, by eye, smile, frown, whisper, mouthing of words, speech, gestures, in rooms filled with oblivious others. At fifteen, I knew a girl with whom I "humped" in various public, though usually unoccupied, places. Once we went to the movies. When we were seated, in the packed theater, she laid her coat over my lap and unzipped my fly. As I clutched with anxiety, and tried to watch the very important film, which had cost me what at that age was a lot of money, she fondled me. Nobody knew. Nobody saw. Nobody kicked us out. It is the same, now, when I urinate while in my seat at the theater, movies, opera. One Christmas, a couple of friends gave me a collection of custom-made bags—lined in plastic, zippered, monogrammed—in which to carry my urinal. The collection included a gray flannel bag for downtown daytime use, a seersucker bag for summer, a tiger bag for sexual engagements, and a black velvet bag for the opera. At the end of an opera one evening, the woman I was with took my urinal, in its black velvet bag, to the ladies' room to dump it. On her way back to me, with my wheelchair, she placed the zipped-up bag containing the emptied urinal on the cushion of the chair while she wheeled it down the aisle. Arriving at my seat, she informed me, with hilarious amazement, that the bag—evidently while she was looking about her—had been swiped. We imagined the thief, on the street, greedily unzipping the elegant black velvet, monogramed evening purse. No one can be sure what's in anything, what anything is. Anything is possible.

My own peculiarly intense interest in what people are doing, what they are like, behind doors, foreheads, beneath clothes, in the dark, goes way back. The preoccupation, which I think of as literary, is an altered version of my parents' profession of psychiatry, and in part a consequence of my parents' practicing psychiatry. A feature of the shared family knowledge as I grew up was that patients weren't discussed. The substance of what my parents did, much more interesting than what most parents did, was hidden from me. The writer, thrilled by the odor of secrets, is nosy. The writer tends to peel—often discovering absolutely nothing—what appears to be from what is or may be; tends to remember that the public, the formal, the social, is often only a version of a room or a person or a brain, that neatness is revised messiness; or will suspect that messiness is revised neatness. Forever nosy, I have always been nosy about how others see me, what, if anything, they imagine about me, and, if they are looking at all, whether they see through me to see me looking to see whether they are looking. After the accident, having become a drama containing mysteries, in place of an actor, I gained justification for my interest in the interest of others in me. As much as some people need to suppose me restricted, dependent—so that they may love down, or count themselves lucky, or to avoid the confusion that my physical state presents, or to avoid worrying about me (if dependent, then I am taken care of)—others wonder and worry about the relation between what I appear to them to be and what I may be, or may not be. Not only "How did you get here?" and "Are you busy enough?" but Does he live alone? How does he get food? Can he cook? How does he get dressed? Given that he's in that wheelchair, can he stand? How does he go to the bathroom? Can he take a shower? A bath? Is he clean? Does he have a girlfriend? Sex? How does he have sex? Is he married? Was he married? Can he have children? Does he? Was it polio? An auto accident? Was he driving? Is he in pain? Does he like the attention? I fear a woman I am with for the first time thinking: he says he was slow getting into this taxi with me because he is tired and has had a little too much to drink. Is he justifying his slowness because, in fact, he is always this slow? Does he tire easily? Is the "a little too much to drink" meant to justify the fatigue?

If I were not "in a wheelchair," some of these are—or these are some of—the questions I suppose I would ask myself, or others, about someone like me, or would ask someone like me, if it were appropriate (though I do not know whether, were I not in a wheelchair, I would allow myself to be curious about, or want to become close to, someone in a wheelchair, particularly a woman; I do not know only because I am in a wheelchair). These are questions I imagine people have asked themselves about me, or questions that they have asked me, or have asked others believed to know me well enough to answer them. Many people who know me best don't know minor important things about me, because, knowing well what I am able to do, they infer the rest of it without thinking, or because they (like most strangers) want to leave my privacy alone, or because what is important to them about me is what I show and say (and ask). It is to those most able to take me physically for granted that I am most likely to report scenes of physical failure: falling; dropping eggs; a plate of spaghetti sliding from my lap; the oozing from my arms of a huge, dispersing manuscript, which I slowly, too calmly, collect from the floor, restore to sequence, and drop again; losing my grip on my wheels at the steep bottom of the Guggenheim Museum's long, curling ramp, down which I had casually been taking myself while viewing the paintings—losing my grip, shouting "Watch out!" as I sledded into the rear, fortunately fleshy, of a woman walking ahead of me, clipping her to the lobby floor. Telling such anecdotes can relieve me, if they make others laugh, or if I know I won't be overly defined in the anecdotes' terms. I have come more and more to like being candid about what's embarrassing, frustrating, complicated for me, minor or major, inside and out, and less and less to imagine (as I did most busily at the dangerous end of my first life and the dangerous beginning of my second) that I am beyond the need for candor, that there is nothing to be candid about, that everything is fine, fine. The less I talked about difficulty, the less difficulty there was and the less difficult I felt myself to be. Those I trust trust me with their candor, about themselves, about me. Friends will sing "Happy Birthday" to me, followed by "Stand up, Stand up," or they will make a raucous issue, before many guests, over a few peas I may have spilled beneath a dinner table, and I will be shocked into belly laughter. Friends, friendly people, understand that I can, in the least ashamed way, see myself as susceptible to comic interpretation or treatment, as I sometimes am, like sex and funerals. Such people are also able to understand that my insufficiences and inefficiencies are not exclusively accountable to my remaining paralysis— that I possess conventional weaknesses, and queer weaknesses having nothing to do with the results of the accident—and, seeing me entire, mock any of my mockabilities. I once received, as birthday gifts, from a network of loving mockers, approximately three dozen copies of *War and Peace*, in many editions, including Russian, French, Spanish, and Japanese, as well as English, because I had not read the book. Overknown, misknown, I am also perfectly known.

I go for my friends' weaknesses—baldness, compulsions, affectations, ignorance, excessively indicated knowledge, competitiveness, hypochrondria, overconfidence, underconfidence—and they do not, evidently, take my doing so as cripple-bitter (oh, Brickner said that because he isn't or doesn't or can't—though I believe that I have developed a bent for regarding the behavior of people I do not know well, or like much, according to weakness: I see their lives as marginal when they may be simply lives; and I am always smelling rationalization). My friends and I generally share an understanding that teasing means an expansion of the possibilities for loving attention. Teasing notices and it remembers. A mockable feature of any one of us becomes a constantly recalled motif in our spoken book. It is possible to love, in a friend, what offends. Most of what's funny is not funny in its original state, but pathetic, foolish, embarrassing, peculiar, painful. One learns that pathos is not in every case to be handled tactfully or pain always to be revered, that hooking an exposed frailty, or that a cool response to a swollen response, can signify health, love.

We have all by now, though, suffered in ways none of us wants to hook, and none of us can cool for one another; suffered through dangerous illness, indefinitely arid marriages or careers, through divorces, bankruptcy, insanity, disastrous automobile accidents, the death of children or mates, brothers, sisters, parents, the dearest of friends—the death of people who, already, will never come back to us. If I was the first to suffer (if suffering is what to call it), then most of the people I know have caught up with me, or learned kinds of pain I will never know, and I have surpassed myself through experiencing the death of others. I am no longer the marked one, even while I continue to be the one alive, among my friends, most touched by direct physical damage. I am now only one peculiarity of experience among many different kinds. It has taken a while for what I—others may not—think of as the dimming of my accident-made uniqueness to occur. And it has taken me longer to notice the dimming. For years I have been the *continuing* evident drama. My particular uniqueness is defined partly by permanence and partly by being overt. The peculiarizing drama in the life of each friend, much as it may be memorable, does not cling as mine does. I am it. But if I am the only one among us in a wheelchair, my friends, too, have bodies. My friends, too, have intimate physical difficulties, awkwardnesses, restraints, similar to mine, other, perhaps worse, than mine, ailments that I will never suffer, far greater frequency of illness, "their own problems." The years leak secrets. Others have lived secrets I never imagined, are right now living secrets I cannot imagine. Early in the second decade of my second life, I passed through a moment of revelation that I had already passed through early in the second decade of my first life, as most people do. The moment said, again: you are not the center; everyone is.

Others, too, had been or would be going to bed with other people's wives or husbands. But I wasn't imagining it specifically of them anymore than—I supposed—they were of me. For all my alertness to secrecy, I spent little time hypothesizing what went on behind my friends' lives. For all my love of poker, I spent little time analyzing the cards and odds around me. Most of my friends were already married. I assumed, as if adultery were for the single, that they had all their sex at home. I assumed they assumed of me that I was having none, and that many of them had decided (were they thinking about me at all?) that I couldn't or—through fear or tact—wouldn't. Where was my woman? I was unable to tell them, or even to protest too much that I had one. I wondered what others wondered about me rather as if I were the only one among us with secrets to protect.

In October 1962, my novel, *The Broken Year,* was published. Sarah and I celebrated in bed. Doubleday gave me a party. My mother attended, to my pride. I felt my father's absence. I had something to show him.

Shortly following my publication, the Cuban missile crisis, as it was known to those less concerned than I with my book's fate, threatened the life of *The Broken Year.* Soviet ships moved for days toward a collision with our blockade. I was angry, as if robbed of headlines and, potentially, of future. If the collision occurred, the world went up. A writer, at publication, wants to control the world, arrange the book's reception. I would not sell my seventy-five thousand copies with people thinking about world-wide death, and if world-wide death took place, nobody left would feel like reading. And I wouldn't be left. I moved about as if I were tiptoeing. My muscles were queasy. I could smell the fallout. Death had not been palpable to me in the hospital, but it was now; I had time to imagine it. At the most suspenseful point of the crisis, when Khrushchev replied in bellicose form to a Kennedy cable, and it looked as though this were actually it, the end of us all, the end of my inch-long career, I went to another party, where, after two drinks, I vomited into a tureen.

When the crisis, amazingly, had dissolved, and the world resumed its business, I waited again for the publicity that would make *The Broken Year* a household phrase beyond my mind's household. I received altogether fewer than two dozen reviews, many of them tepid, most of them brief, some a tiny paragraph, or from distinctively minor newspapers. It became necessary for me to take support from the antagonistic critics. My book provoked more dramatically than it pleased. Bruno Mc-Andrew, O.S.B., of St. Anselm's Abbey, Washington, D.C., in

Best Sellers, a review journal whose title couldn't help me: "This is the first novel of a young New York Jew . . . love affairs . . . handled in such a way as to put the book in the partly objectionable class . . . wallows in such sensual descriptions that it would not be unfair to characterize it as decadent literature." (With three inexplicit sexual scenes I was D. H. Lawrence.) And F. Gardner Clough, in the Newburgh, New York, *Orange County Post:* ". . . a character that should never have been born in the first place . . . the cooked-up account of a paralytic. Too morbid for me, thank you." I could enjoy a favorable review in the *Book-of-the-Month Club News* because it would be widely read and because the critic concluded, "As a first novel, moreover, it is a far cry from the usual overwritten, overwrought examples of the breed. Alive, tart, it is the real thing in the annals of contemporary, middle-middle-class, urban adolescence." These words praised me right where I wanted praise. This review was my rave. Otherwise, the enthusiastic reviews were being read, I began to fear, by so few book-buyers that the Cuban missile crisis was going to be irrelevant. For all my grandiosity of expectation, I did not come near to being depressed. Evidently, I was, or fell back on being, happy to publish a novel, at under thirty. Now that the world was going to stay, my career had life. And my friends admired the book. What upset me instead was the busybody insistence, in three appreciative, minor notices, on straightening out the relation between me and the character of Eric Green, as if my novel were a lie it would benefit readers to expose. Two of the reviews referred to my automobile accident. Why, they seemed to be asking, if Brickner had an auto accident, did Eric Green fall downstairs to break his neck? They weren't going to let me get away with it. What would have made sense in an article or interview, in which I might have talked about the ways in which I had fed episodes of my life into Eric Green's imagined story, had no place in a review of my novel. My life wasn't being reviewed. The third, the crudest, of the pieces, gossiped like a right-wing fanatic grabbing for a slippery Communist: "Although there is no mention on the book's jacket that this is an autobiography [quite true] Brickner's former classmates at Columbia U. might well suspect it is because he had always been confined to a wheelchair while attending there." (The novel did not return Eric to college.) This one, to whose author prose was furniture in a strange, dark room, added insult by calling my prose "superb." I did not know these writers, or how they knew about me. Their personal comments threatened my imagination's public strength and flexibility. They were strangers presuming from a new distance.

I intended my published imagination to be my public manhood, a conspicuous accomplishment setting me apart from nonwriters and from unpublished writers I knew, and setting me apart from my crippled self. To have written about a crippled person resembling—but not—me was flirtatious, but less flirtatious, I had felt, than literarily courageous. The more richly I could make up a character so much and so little like me as Eric was, the more remarkable my book would have to be, the more respectfully regarded. It was as if I wanted stranger-readers to know of the resemblances between me and Eric so that they could see the astonishing differences; as if I wanted to be a magician performing the book's composition in front of them as they read.

So, too, I wanted to impress strangers with my wheelchair presence in such a way that they would think: how magically easy he makes his difficulties—how much unlike his wheelchaired self he is, rather than: how difficult it must be for him—how much the way he looks, wheelchaired, his life must be. I wanted my powers of conversion recognized. I wanted my difficulties acknowledged and I wanted them forgotten, both. For my novel as for myself, I wanted a readership sufficiently imaginative to assume imagination of me—fictional imagination, physical imagination, fictional, physical, flexibility: artistry. But I had asked for it, asked for assumptions about my novel as much as, without asking, I asked for them by appearing in my wheelchair in public. I tempted—and I will never be able not to tempt—

invasion. My novel, like me, asked of the reader, the stranger, too much distance and too much interest, too much precise, immediate interpretation.

The novel was sold to television, the *Alcoa Premiere* drama series on ABC. The night of the show, in April, 1963, a few friends, along with my mother (it was somewhat as if she were finally going to witness my accident), came to my apartment to watch. Fred Astaire, *Alcoa Premiere*'s "Host," stood on the landing of Eric's stairs to introduce the program. Please don't dance, Fred. I gazed at the stairs every bit as intensely as if they were the real stairs filmed, brought back to me, the real stairs down which Eric had fallen, the real stairs I had made up, more real now to me than the road. Otherwise, the program struck me as not having needed my novel for its story, the adapter had so altered and simplified the novel. Indeed, the play was so simple as to make me feel like a master of fictional density. The Nielsen rating for the show was 16.5 million viewers. Of the seventy-five thousand people I had anticipated buying the novel—I had stuck with seventy-five thousand to present my getting carried away—fewer than fifteen hundred bought it.

From Sarah I expected permanence. She warned me against insisting we were permanent, or demanding the promise of permanence from her, not because she planned ever to leave us but because to expect permanence implied human control of destiny. She was not God; she could not promise; and she refused to think of anything as permanent. I could not help it. She meant permanence. We were never going to be over. Sarah was "with me," was "there," even more than I imagined her to be. She knew me precisely. If I thought her oblivious to something I said, or meant, I would later be surprised to learn that she had heard everything and added her own thinking to it. She remembered me. For Sarah to say, "You said—" made memory seem a new invention for connecting people, like the telephone. How did it work? I was amazed. I lived in her brain. I had spent thirty years being known and remembered and never wondered how. I felt that in Sarah's brain I had an extra life. If I thought she had forgotten something, it usually turned out, by proof, that it was I who had forgotten. It gave me peace to be wrong. If she was right, she was there.

She was there, but pursuable, permanently pursuable. She went away daily. At night I became a widower for the rest of my life. I noticed that only moonlight kept me company, and I thought how single, alone, the moonlight found me, how much like an open-air grave it made my double bed. I played, there, the game of Would She Return? like Tristan waiting for his cure. We always started again at the beginning. She always returned, reached me, got to me, needed me, her face comfort, her brain trustworthy, various, confirming, receptive, self-sustaining, her body, each time, the same shocking new secret, and a source of mysterious energy, heating my heart to semen. Sarah uncontrolled me. In the final instants before the stuff spurted out of me, it boiled like a force that could knock people on their backs. Now, ten years after Margaret, I enjoyed the power; danger felt like safety. I enjoyed the universal sensation: the squeezed squirming, the bubbly itching, the effervescent pressure of lust about to let go.

I needed more permanence from Sarah. We had to get married. I had to have her where I couldn't lose her. Every month or so, I asked her when she thought we would marry. We talked, dotingly and practically, about what it would be like, how cozy it would be (I would bring her food in bed, she would want to just stay home and be with me), what our children would be like, where we would live, what we would do for enough money. After Doubleday, I'd collected unemployment insurance (taking a cab weekly to the insurance office). Since then, aside from the Doubleday advance, which equaled about five months of my quite modest financial life, my mother had been supporting me, paying for graduate school, as she nicely thought of it. The money from the TV show—what Doubleday hadn't applied against that part of their advance to me that my book sales had left uncompensated—I was saving. It wasn't enough for anything but an emergency or a luxury.

Sarah wanted to, was going to, marry me. She agreed we had to get married. It would be a terrible waste if we didn't. We belonged together. I must understand that a life for her worth living depended on me, my tenderness, the unique energy of my interest in her, the expressions of her personality and body I made possible, desirable. She was as lonely at night as I. Lonelier. But she couldn't just dump her husband. She didn't love him but she didn't dislike him. When? When? Soon. Soon. In the meantime, we must enjoy each other, she warned me. If I brooded too much on what we didn't have, if I was unhappier than I was happy, then she couldn't stay.

I had to value her unwillingness to dump her husband. What she wouldn't do to him she wouldn't do to me. Sarah was generous. If she were not generous, she would dump him. If she were not generous, she would not love me so wholly, at such inconvenience and risk to her life, even though I was myself much of her convenience and her life. Yet, my need for her aside, might it not be selfish of her to need me while protecting her husband from pain, to give me only part of herself, the away part, even though she called my apartment her home, when I was giving her more than myself? I had begun another novel: whenever Sarah could be with me, I quit work. But wasn't it selfish of me to demand more of her than she was already giving?

If I had money, would I have any more of her sooner? I suspected that she wanted to live as she lived, even with him, "comfortably," while waiting to see whether I, by my writing—which she would not allow me to give up for a salaried job, were I able to find one—could make enough money to combine with hers for continuing comfort and the eventual support of a child. When I did not feel Sarah was honoring me with her hope that I would hit a jackpot with the next novel or the one after that, I

accused her, to myself, of humoring me in my writing career in order to forestall our marriage. If I continued to write, we would be likely never to have enough money, and likely never to know how much we might have. She did not really want to marry me; she expected I would one day drop the subject. Was she, then, also humoring me about not having sex with her husband? How could she avoid sex with him? She was too desirable. They lived alone together at night, on weekends, in the same apartment. (She had drawn me the apartment.) It wasn't that difficult, she explained. He wasn't that interested. Was she lying to me, avoiding him only as often as she dared, or asking for him when my penis had failed her on a given day, or when I had shoved her, by pestering, into affection for him? Was she lying to prevent my leaving her (while he, infuriatingly—loyally?—refused to leave her despite her sexual spurning)? Did he *know* about our intimacy and condone her part in it as a good deed, their good deed? Was she lying because she suffered having dutiful sex with him, and wanted to spare me her anguish? She could tell me, I said, she must tell me. I could take it. But I didn't say that, were it true, she couldn't tell me, she mustn't. It was as if I kept the subject alive because to learn she was having sex with him would be to know I wasn't depriving him. I wanted reason to be jealous. If she gave me reason, then I wouldn't be guilty. But if she gave me reason, I would have to give her up, because she had been lying. I went to a performance of *King Lear*. Lear, failing to understand his daughter's honest love, and entering madness, sits with his fool. The fool devotedly tries to ease Lear's desperation, and educate him out of it, with a riddle: "Thou canst tell why one's nose stands i' th' middle on's face?" Lear: "No." Fool: "Why, to keep one's eyes of either side's nose, that what a man cannot smell out, 'a may spy into." Lear: "I did her wrong." At this, I sobbed.

Trust her, Sarah pleaded. Love her. Look how lucky we were, both in love for the first time, and with one another, both having waited, both having arrived. Perfect timing, perfect coincidence. Here we were, at last, with everything the other needed. Nothing was wrong. Do not make it wrong.

When I needed consolation for being in love with her, unable to bear fidelity to another man's wife, unable (forgetting the power) to bear the powerlessness of loving her—my desire could arrange nothing; all movement, all decisions, daily and for the future, were hers to make—I would find a woman to embrace in a spasm of misery that looked like passion, to lie down with, to undress, then to disappoint, telling her I was in love. My penis, in any case, lay flaccid in fidelity, as if absent Sarah were its exclusive puppeteer. I tried to punish Sarah for loving me by confusing the expectations of other women. I punished myself while saving myself, by failing to betray her. If I failed with others, I proved Sarah was not unfaithful to me. Had I succeeded with others, I would have known she was betraying me with her husband. I did not tell her about my coy infidelities. I told her again and again that I could not stand the idea (whose idea?) of not being with her forever.

All Sarah's steady love, drawing out all my love, all we had restored to one another and all we were adding, all our mutual tolerance, our thoroughness of familiarity, our breathing of one another, our mutual *incorporation*, gave the fullest health to my life while making me weak, unsteady. Though it was me, not her husband, she loved, it was him, not me, she lived with. Though I knew she loved me, and knew she would always love me, I feared as if fear were knowledge that I would never "win her over." With all I had, I couldn't be sure I had it. To love someone as hard as I was loving Sarah is to hope never to die. Such love is itself death at any moment and permanent life, is life and death in your hands and out of your hands. Having won her, I still had to win her. I had no choice but to pester her to permanence. What else could I do? If I shut up, she would forget her promise to marry me, to save me forever from dying. The change, at the accident, in the route of my life, had brought me to her; but were it not for the accident's subduing of my reach, agility, motility, I would be certain of winning her over, I felt. "Strength" would prevail. Her admiration for my strength I dismissed or ignored in hasty modesty. What with Margaret I had imagined to be appropriate, with Sarah I knew to be imperative. We had to realize our ideal. After marriage would come more marriage, longer marriage, marriage forever, permanent permanence, time taking us along. Progress, always starting again at the beginning, future, the endless expanding of future, was the way I conceived of safety. Such anxious ambitions are among the common secrets of love, and all the more common to the particularly dangerous kind of love we had undertaken. Sarah, too, gazed on our permanence, with her less desperate eyes and for her peculiar reason, that is, her being poorly married. The common secret anxieties of the lover were, at the same time, intensified in the accidental me.

When I follow a peculiar response of mine, I see it reflected, in versions, outside me, in others. When I follow someone else's peculiar response, I become a deep mirror of flesh. I represent. So do we all, each in our peculiar way.

TWELVE

IN THE FALL of 1964, with Dick and Margot Marek, I flew to London. We had tickets to see Laurence Olivier as Othello, a performance whose power had become far-traveling news, like a foreign marvel in an ancient century. Olivier had turned himself into a "Negro," in gait, posture, and voice (having trained it lower). His performance was so intense and exhausting that *Othello* was scheduled in the National Theatre repertory like an opera; Olivier could "sing" only once or twice a week. People slept on line overnight to get standing-room tickets.

Dick and Margot stayed with a friend, I comfortably alone in a hotel whose convenience of layout had been verified for me by a travel agent. The three of us would meet for a matinee of something, have dinner, go to an evening performance of something, separate for the night, and repeat the routine the next day, "approaching" our Saturday afternoon's *Othello*, which stood at the end of the week, still miles away, a colossal mountain, or Victoria Falls, or, for pilgrims, the Pope. The performance had the quality of being thrilling and present even while invisibly distant. Like Sarah.

I did not, this visit, walk around London. I was wheeled, by Dick or in a taxi. But it was adult Sarah I missed, not child-adult Margaret. I was so much stronger from the inside out in 1964 than I'd been on my original trip in 1952 that it was hardly as if I'd been weakened since then. Walking London, my first time there, I'd been estranged from Margaret, and half-paralyzed with fright at what I might have done to her. Twelve years later, despite my constrained legs and lowered height and thinned arms, I felt more efficient getting around the city than I had when nineteen and still normally nerved. I'd leaped the Atlantic in an afternoon. To negotiate the taxis, different from New York's, meant proficiency. In London, I weighed myself. Whatever I had lost between the ages of nineteen and thirty-one, I'd gained more. Otherwise, I wouldn't be there again at all, under the circumstances. Otherwise, there would be no Sarah under my skin; though she could not get letters from me, unlike Margaret, I chatted with her gaily, through my cells, knowing we belonged to one another, knowing that most of our difficulties were necessary, knowing that our love was worth the difficulties, knowing that, however much I suffered from loving her, and however much I suffered more than was necessary, our love was in fact love, that I had learned from her what love felt like. On this trip, I was someone loving a woman whose body and brain shared her intelligence and cheerful intensity, her health. I knew she was happy for me to be in London, and I knew she wished she were with me. I wanted her to know what it felt like to miss the gone-away one. I wanted her to be happy, not miserable, but I wanted her to know. I wanted her happiness to be her knowledge of how much she missed me. I liked what I knew to be the power of my absence. But my vengefulness felt loving.

The Mareks and I reached *Othello*. It began merely as a theater experience much more tense than usual—arrival at the theater, the full darkness, the curtain rising, more portentous than we were used to by now, returning us to the cruciality of our earliest theater-going, when everything we attended was this *Othello*. The black Olivier entered, dressed all in white, carrying a fat red rose, chuckling: a great entrance. What made us suck in our breath was his thrilling calculation. As the play developed, his theatrical dynamics, his playing, continued to be noticeable. But his performance, at its climaxes, always shed his kind of vividness, Olivier beautifully being Othello, to become more than gorgeous acting, more than acting that wasn't acting, more than "believable," and more than, and other than, Othello. He—Olivier, Othello, Othello playing Olivier—at the fullness of his inflamed jealousy, was transformed into Jealousy Raging. From my seat about one-third of the way back in the orchestra, I shied from his noise, and I winced, as if he were screaming at me, as if I had done something terrible to him, as if, gone crazy, or a lion, he might at any moment jump off the stage and invade the audience, killing me and all of us, tearing us apart, continuing to scream. I heard him disbelieving Desdemona *and* us. He was a man waving a gun. I did not melt in his tragedy, I froze against it, I grew ice on my skin, as I had at my father's memorial service, exhibiting an animal's trick saved for peril, like changing color, or squirting ink. The power of the performance was in its literal dangerousness.

In Othello's rage I must have heard the black man's voice, my father awakened too early in the morning, or my father betrayed by me in a way I had never betrayed him. On occasion, in my house, while I was growing up, and while I was growing up there after the accident, doors slamming were sometimes merely doors being closed with force, or with the help of wind. I imagined arguments that weren't taking place, which I had caused. I must have heard, in Othello's rage, my own voice as it would sound if Sarah were to betray me with her husband; and I must have heard the voice of Sarah's husband. Voices I had heard, never heard, answering events that had occurred, never occurred, were blasting my ears.

The Mareks and I ate dinner afterward excited, nervous, exhausted, miserable, as if we had escaped a disaster in which others had been killed, and then went to our last play together. The brutality of the afternoon preoccupied me, and the unexpectedness of the way in which the *Othello* had been great, that it hadn't let me weep, that it had frightened me so directly, that it had not been "perfect," that its deficiencies were ironically related to its strange greatness. Olivier's occasional "brilliance," his visible artfulness, belonged to the natural storm that destroyed it. Perhaps he arranged his synthetic touches as symptoms and analogues of the unreality he killed when he killed Desdemona and his jealous self. Othello has every reason, and none, to expect the fatal outcome of his mixed marriage. From time to time we are reminded that we do not ever know what is going to happen next, to whom, at whose hands. Iago is under Othello's nose. Desdemona is without deceit. Othello is a rock that melts.

The Mareks moved on to Spain. My dear Columbia friend of the *Lady Chatterley's Lover* agreement came and drove me to Cambridge, where he now lived, with his wife and three children, for a three-day visit, an intimate tour of town and university and family life. I used up the last few days of my two-week (economy-fare) trip alone in London, seeing peripheral friends, and friends of friends. Because I was exercising my flexibility, getting myself around the city, managing to keep its geography in focus —because I was *alone in London*—I did not much mind being alone. Sarah's reception, by smile, questions, flesh, and Doubleday's answer to my second novel, which I had completed and handed into them a few weeks before my departure, were not far away. My return home meant excitement, an extension of the energy of my trip's success. But I did not have enough to do. I noticed myself in time and space. Sitting alone in my hotel's lobby, I noticed that the hotel was "wrong" for me; were it not for its physical convenience I would be staying somewhere else, more appropriate to my intrinsic taste, an odder, older, more graceful, less—or more—expensive place, less pervasively populated by German and Japanese businessmen. I had to remind myself that a writer, of all people, must remember that anywhere was interesting, the details of dullness, foreign and domestic, worth noting; that I must treat my limitations as aspects of flexibility, experience—were I not stuck with this hotel, I wouldn't know this hotel; that I must try to avoid typing my surroundings too firmly, as I must try not to fear their typing me; that I must beware of making assumptions, and assuming assumptions.

My second week run out, I took a cab to London Airport, climbed the steps to the plane, and flew home. My mother, who had once said how grateful she was that I'd gotten to England and France before the accident, who had, not long ago, been chauffeuring her ashamed, bristling son to and from school, met me at Kennedy, and drove me to my apartment. At sixty-four, in widowhood, my mother was healthy and busy. The money she gave me she could give without strain—an accomplishment—her psychiatric practice more active than it had ever been. The asthma that had choked her from 1938 to 1951 she was able to keep slack with the use of Cortisone. Though I depended, for the time being, on her money, I did not constrict her life, with filial asthma, as it once appeared I would be doing for as long as we lived. We both had futures. Over both our lives, we had changed, been changed, many times. But no change, finally, had set us back. Gray light, blackness, had never settled on us, as it does, early, for some. I came home to an apartment repainted in my absence, the furniture properly back in place, the telephone ringing as I rolled in the door, Sarah, happy and impatient, calling. Tomorrow together, turning each other inside out. I telephoned my agent—I was a writer, I had an agent. Doubleday had just rejected my new novel.

Over the next year and a half, fifteen publishers turned down *The Lines of Love.* Many of the rejections were respectful, the result of three, four considered, hopeful readings. The book often produced enthusiasm for particular scenes and qualities. It was felt to be effectively erotic, the leading female character to be complex and well understood, the dialogue and description original and lively. The writing put one editor in mind of F. Scott Fitzgerald. But no one loved the book, and some hated it. The novel was about a love affair between an acting student, Peter, and Emily (not married), an editor who quits a trendy publishing house (altogether unlike Doubleday); their estrangement, caused by a dilemma of Emily's for which Peter is in part responsible; and their reuniting. The strings of the story—blackmail, lying, counterlying, the tight interconnection of many characters—were so numerous and so crossed that I often frowned sorting them out for myself. I had wanted, this time, to be sure to write what nobody would dare doubt was a novel, what nobody could think of calling autobiographical. Little did they know; almost as little did I. The accumulated objections to the book were that Peter reacted out of proportion to his difficulties as a lover of Emily and as an actor, that he was less sinned against than he imagined; and that the victories of the book's ending—his return to Emily, his winning of a part in a (bad) Broadway play—were too quick, were glib. Also, Peter thought too much, didn't act enough. For all its plot, the book was not decisively dramatic. Over the period of its rejection, I myself came to reject it, for the reasons of others and for reasons behind their reasons that they couldn't see. I slowly recognized the book as a swollen conspiratorial plan for the betrayal, by Emily as Sarah, of me as Peter. There was too much plotting in the plot. The novel wasn't "true." Its excessive complexity and ineffectiveness were the consequence of its falsifying origins. With its over-happy ending I had tried to compensate for its over-anxious story. I withdrew the novel from circulation before it had run out of well-regarded publishing houses.

In any case, by the spring of 1965, I had started another novel, much larger than *The Lines of Love*, yet hidden in a corner of it. What I came to call *Bringing Down the House* also hid more of me than *The Lines of Love* had. The thicker the fiction, the greater privacy a writer has to be personal. I didn't finish finding myself in *Bringing Down the House* until long after I had finished writing it. I am all through it, my most intimate cells, in its characters, its story, its meanings, in its very thickness of protection, more of me than in either of the first two novels. More of me, less visible. In the novel, an eminent American playwright attempts to destroy a mammoth culture center recently erected in "the heartland of Artland," the geographical center (according to land mass) of the United States, Butte County, South Dakota. The novel was set in 1973, but by 1965 the country was already stuffing itself on the unintelligent seriousness and frivolous brutality of its spreadingly popular high art. At the New York theater, the audiences were like boosters of cheap pessimism, the pompous, and the hostile. Two or three works each by Albee, John Osborne, the middle Arthur Miller, the middle Tennessee Williams, made me as gloomy and irritable as one feels during an argument it is impossible to win even though one is right. The plays depressed me not with what was in them but with what wasn't. These same plays agreed with those around me. (Later, it would be Pinter's *The Birthday Party; Rosencrantz and Guildenstern Are Dead; Home; Equus,* and other razzle-dazzle duds.) What accounted for the difference I felt between me (and Sarah and a few friends and a few critics) and "the public"? My separateness agitated me; and all the more because it was now clear to me that what I smelled at the theater was not my "superiority" of suffering but the rotting of seriousness on the stage. Serious theater was now *self*-serious, or abject or snappish, but not serious. It did not *teach.* It scared me now in the wrong ways—for the defeat it loved, for the defeat it had become for me, because it was not mine. I did not belong in my own home. I felt anarchistic rage, contempt, for the plays, the audience, but lacked the anarchist's temperament. I was a relative of the audience, perhaps a nephew, certainly too much a good boy to boo what they cheered, or to boo them for cheering, no less plant bombs in their playhouses. Yet, I kept, and have kept, going to plays. Living imitation attracts youth, actual youth and permanent youth. I have kept going to plays in the hope, among other hopes, of "staying" young (and retroactively avoiding the accident).

By the beginning of the sixties, suffering on the stage had begun to sound like propaganda. The difference between Blanche

DuBois's last line in *A Streetcar Named Desire,* which I saw in 1948—"Whoever you are—I have always depended on the kindness of strangers"—and the last lines of *Who's Afraid of Virginia Woolf?,* which I saw in 1963—"Who's afraid of Virginia Woolf. ..." "I ... am ... George. ... I ... am. ..."—is the difference between a tragic tragic pose and a posed tragic pose. If *Who's Afraid of Virginia Woolf?* had been my youth's *Streetcar,* I do not believe it would have handed me my compassion, as *Streetcar* did. It lacks the generosity. I resented the difference. I resented the resentment on the stage. It seemed inaccurate to me. Was *I* inaccurate—short on experience? Did the resentment tempt me? I resented the ease, the pleasure, with which the audience gave in, could afford to give in, to the giving in. They were praising doom. At the theater, the playwrights were telling us, with all the energy it takes to write plays, that we shouldn't have bothered to come to the theater, it wasn't worth it: God isn't coming; the Virginia Woolf is coming; there is "menace" in the air; or Hamlet has the big part, while Rosencrantz and Guildenstern, we, "the little people" of the audience, are manipulated bystanders, "extras"; or the sole alternative to the passionate commitment of murder is to be a "plastic" member of society, a "cipher." (Little wonder such a lesson makes slaves feel good.)

I was no longer part of the audience. I did not want to be them, but I wanted them to be me. My rage made me conspicuous, unsafe. I did not want to disagree with so many strangers—majority was authority—but I couldn't help myself; and it excited me to disagree with so many strangers. It was dangerous, but necessary, to do so. I lived somewhere between Blanche DuBois and the audience. Everybody does, more or less; I more. If strangers didn't aid me when I needed them to—doormen helping me up steps, cabdrivers putting my wheelchair into cabs and taking it out, pedestrians helping cabdrivers and doormen help me into my wheelchair if I fell onto the street getting out of a cab—my selfhood was endangered. Disagreement with strangers risked the withdrawal of their support, and it tested my freedom from them.

The pleasure, lasting three years, of constructing *Bringing Down the House* became conspicuous among my recitable pleasures of either life. My book was a marvel so enormous and intricate that I could not imagine a human being having imagined it. (At the same time, who was *I* to have done so?) I was always looking upward, and around me, for miles, amazed, at the powerful, dense girders of my structure. From a long, bright frieght-train of a dream I scooped, day after day after day, the necessary ideas, plot-connections, scenes, six-dozen characters, voices, mannerisms, jokes, clothes, cars, roads, domiciles, furnishings, skies. I got material by mail and telephone as well, accumulating a large cartonful of glamorously useful maps, photographs, brochures, census figures, industrial and agricultural information. The writing of *Bringing Down the House* was an advanced, prolonged form of what children call playing.

By the time I finished the novel, in the spring of 1968, Sarah and I had finished six years of love. Our longevity was our child. I felt mature, healthily tough, weather-beaten. I was developing muscles of behavior, learning that I had a repertoire of resiliencies, that I was not limited to one famous solo: coming back from the accident. My accident was not my only accident. But I could handle the others, handle them *also:* a difficult, crucial love; one unsuccessful novel; and one rejected novel, from which future would now emerge. I felt versatile. I had many hands. I was capable of as much as, or more than, but not less than, others. I was capable of Sarah, of novels, of the city, of friends, of coming, of keeping my own house, capable of myself.

This time, the world, not the book, would be wrong if the book weren't published. My agent, and experienced friends, had no doubt the book would be bought. Thus, when the rejections added up to three, four, objectivity consolidating, I was readier to be angry than I had been over the experience of the last novel, and readier to be frightened. The world could be wrong, and I could remain unpublished. The rejections, always laboriously taking their time, taking mine while they were at it, weeks, months for each announcement, continued to arrive, asking me what to do with them. My agent sent me copies of the embroidered zeroes. "Impressed as I am . . . there's an enormous amount of work to do on this sprawling manuscript . . . belabored as I am. . . . Mr. Brickner interests me enormously. . . . Please do allow me to see more work of Brickner's, and do please let him know of my admiration for his wit and originality, and for his own very unique way of looking at things." ". . . the incredible brilliance of much of his writing. . . . There is a book here, held down perhaps by an uncontrolled genius. Talent is all over the place, and so are finely achieved effects." There was nothing to fight, nothing to fight with. I was not the kind to go downtown and yell in the faces of these torturing admirers. Was it the audience I despised retaliating genteely? I had a poisonously saddening dream in which I picked up a rifle, shrugged, and let it drop. At dinner parties, I would look at friends, and think: they have caught up with me, passed me, sold their second books. My question could only be: what was wrong with me? Others got the world's say-so, and got it repeated on request at the Bureau of Publication. I thought of myself as seated not in my wheelchair but in an armchair, the world's kind of chair. The armchair was deep, and its back slanted backward at forty-five degrees; my own arms, in this fantasy, stopped at the bottom of my shoulders. I couldn't get out of the armchair. I was stuck in it. I sat in it, but I didn't belong in it.

After twenty years of smoking, I decided to give up cigarettes. I had first smoked to inhale in my first season of summer stock, at sixteen. When my parents came to visit me, I told my father, a heavy smoker, that I had started smoking in order to "emancipate myself"—from him, we both understood. He laughed, in a sweet, startled manner, and said, "If you think that by smoking you're emancipating yourself from anything, you're crazy." Two years later, he gave up his cigarettes, to save his heart. Five years later, having had to quit after my accident, I started again, sneaking my smokes at home, from packs friends brought me. I told Gurewitsch. He gave me permission, "considering my other frustrations." I told my father what Gurewitsch had said. My father listened, saying nothing. Now, at thirty-six, to save my heart, I had to quit for the rest of my life. My friends who had quit and my friends who still smoked would admire me. I would admire me. My family, including my dead father, would admire me. The cancer, for which the accident had originally been a decoy, was coming. Repeatedly, intentionally, I imagined myself going to my doctor for a check-up. Leaving his office. Sunny spring day. Park Avenue. Smart trees on the sidewalk, boutonnieres of trees. Yellow cabs. A movie scene shot on location. An urban version of my accident day. Not the kind of day when bad things happen. My doctor has told me I have incurable cancer. I go home, in one of the pretty yellow cabs, to my home, with the news, alone. For months I scared myself with this sunny green-and-yellow scene outside my doctor's office, telling myself it could be, just as it could be that your third novel will be rejected all the way down the line. (And you will not, in reason, be able to write a fourth.) You did not know you were going to break your neck, either. If I quit smoking, saved myself, I remained worth saving; and if I quit smoking, I erased the equation of cancer and the book's death. I quit smoking, cold, one weekend. My book continued to die anyway.

My accident had been a success; it had made me. It had unrolled yards of years of optimism before me. But for two novels, five years' work, to be ignored, would be burial I had no way to resist. I was only now getting my share of "life itself," "hard knocks." This was it—everybody's danger, future shriveling and changing color in one's fingers. Thirty-six was an age when lives got decided. At the same time, privately, I thought: after "all I've been through"? Don't I deserve a break? My book, by itself, deserves a break, but don't I? Anger settled in my lungs. I used irritability on my friends as if I were angry with them. My mouth learned a curve of mournful disgust.

In 1967, I had met, at the Mareks, a writer named Mark Mirsky, who was starting up a program at City College in which writers, rather than teachers, would teach some sections of freshman composition, entirely according to methods of their choice. Mirsky hired me on the spot, at dinner, because he liked the confidence of my views on fiction. So I had become a teacher, and was good at it, good at using my power, which had been presented to me, like new equipment. With it, I answered questions—having answers is power; I gave advice, support, ideas, caused the dumb to speak and subdued the noisy; I corrected; I praised; I was responsible for many; I marked; when I was funny, I got a large family's laughter; I was alert under pressure, seizing fast chances to grab a point, a point, it might be, I had never seen before. I was at ease and I was excited. Teaching, I found, stood for several kinds of freedom: the chance to express myself at will; to learn and negotiate a new part of the city; to deal with kinds of people I had never known, would never have known, of an age my age doubled; and to make money. Teaching, I was earning more than I needed to live on. I stopped taking money from my mother, I replaced her accomplishment with my own.

Since 1959, I had been writing humor pieces, book reviews, and occasional articles for newspapers and magazines. I was read by thousands and millions. I could read myself where, growing up, I had read others. My life, on the evidence, was no cause for shame. But teaching, reviewing, writing articles—for all their value and repute, and for all their implication that I could manage in everybody's world—were limbs off a torso if I could not get a second book published. To have published one book left me—the body of me—behind, stranded in time, embarrassed. To have published one book, a book I would not have written had it not been for my peculiarizing accident, meant I wasn't "a writer." To have published one book would be equivalent to having come in Sarah once. Once didn't count. It was as if to do what others did—even to do what some others wanted to do but didn't or couldn't—teach, write for famous newspapers and journals—was not enough for me to do because too many could do it. I had to be rare in the world to make my physical rareness disappear. To equal others, I had to be more than they. I started lower. And the average better-than-ordinary boiled down to nothing on me. I needed a distinct distinction, of a kind others sought. My own distinct distinction—my accident, even my survival, even my successful determination to be a member of the conventional world—was too much a matter not of my doing, too much a matter of luck, of the world's cooperation. I needed a distinction more common than what my accident had provided me, but not so common that the world didn't single out those who reached it, such as "writers." After two years of trying, I had not been able to sell *Bringing Down the House*. I was too short, my arms were too short.

Sarah had not left her husband for me. I could not get us published. Our secrecy had tired me. I hung onto her, but I had begun insistently to imagine letting go of her, falling, eyes shut, taking my chances that I would land on something soft instead of cracking my head open. I was slipping. I had hauled myself back up to her before, but I hadn't slipped so far from her before. It might be easier, now, to drop. On the ground I might find what I needed, if I didn't already have everything I would ever have. I had got used to Sarah. I was frightened, now, of a future of familiarity. Coziness had become the threat of burial. I had swallowed the infinite. The finite was full. I had stopped suffering. I had stopped beginning again. I had stopped waiting, in passion, for Sarah's returns, or her permanent return. I didn't want to marry her any longer, and if I didn't want to marry her I didn't want to remain with her unmarried to her. I had been a bachelor for too long, single with her, half-single. I wanted, therefore, to *be* single, to be what I had become. I "wanted my freedom." I no longer felt freed by Sarah. Whatever she had done for me, and however much I might still love her, it was as if she had kept me from the world, more than the world had kept her from me. I had been *getting* permanence from Sarah. I hated her for the partial kind she had given us, for having given me time to see that if, now—supposing I were making useful money as a writer, or even that I had a tenured position as a teacher, which I didn't—she said, "I am going to get a divorce now, and marry you," I would say, with barely enough breath, "Don't. I can't." (Yet, if I had sold *Bringing Down the House* in 1968 or 1969, wouldn't I have wanted more than ever to marry her, success insisting on success?) But shouldn't our love have made failure bearable? Could our love be called a failure? What more could I ask of it than what it had given me? Completion? What was that? Completion was finished. I was finished. I was out of hope, out of energy, out of guilt, out of jealousy, out of excitement, out of faith, and out of doubt.

Time is always changing direction, force, color, shape, its mind, but it was truer than our longevity, our proved love. Time is truer than anything people can say or think or do. Sarah herself had warned me against trusting to permanence. I, of all people, should have believed her. I, in particular, couldn't. I had wanted no more accidents. I had tried to turn Sarah into still time. Now I was sick of time. "Time only knows the price we have to pay," writes Auden; and "Time will say nothing but I told you so."

When Sarah returned to me from a vacation with her husband in the early summer of 1970, I told her, as if I were saying that I had a cold, that I could no longer continue with her. I didn't say, "Marry me, or I'll quit." She didn't say, "Don't quit, I'll marry you." She said she thought I made sense. She left my apartment. We talked on the phone, almost as if nothing had happened. We met again and talked. We were rare, she reminded me. No one had better love, loved better, than we. I cried hard, as she had taught me to—part of the cure. I cried hardest seeing her cry—she had almost never cried—my body curling as if hot cigarettes were being pressed to my skin. I had gotten to her. I was hurting her. Sobbing, I watched her losing me. She was me. She left.

THIRTEEN

IN DECEMBER of 1970, after months of consideration, Scribner's—publisher of Henry James, Edith Wharton, Thomas Wolfe, F. Scott Fitzgerald, Ernest Hemingway—purchased *Bringing Down the House.* No throwing up of belabored hands over a "sprawling manuscript"; no reverential complaints over its "uncontrolled genius," "incredible brilliance." Rather, a sheaf of precise and creative notes from my new editor, Norman Kotker, a novelist himself. A dozen doctors had by now told me I was dying. Diagnosis, indeed, was killing me. Kotker told me there was nothing wrong that I couldn't fix in a matter of months. I had found Kotker, in effect, as I had once found Sarah, far into a wilderness of humans. At a party on New Year's Eve, sitting beside Lizzie and her husband, she and I long since again friends, I said to her, suddenly weeping, that my life had been saved. I revised *Bringing Down the House* through April, finding answers to Kotker's questions and to new questions of my own. The book went into production, and came out in January of 1972, its jacket by Koren. I had my second novel. I was given a party. A writer, finally, I sat by the door in my wheelchair, kissing and shaking hands with arriving guests. My bar-mitzvah, one of them said.

To be my female accomplishment at the party, I'd invited to join me a woman I'd met not many weeks before. We had spent three or four evenings together, lain down once, remaining clothed, on her uncomfortable couch. We had not threatened love or need. She was colorful, independent, funny, also free (divorced). She took care of her children, held down a large job. I admired her. But in the time between my asking her to the party and the party, I had become uncomfortable with her. We were not meant for each other. We had no future. I did not want to know her better, owe her. She had asked me for nothing, but if she asked for me, and I didn't want her to have me, how would I escape? Only my voice could run. I feared the surrender of choice. If I gave up choice, or if it were taken, I had to pay for its return. And so I wanted to have nothing to do with the woman at all. At the party, I ignored her until she challenged me, then ignored her again. The best thing about us was that we hadn't gone to bed.

Sarah's cure had not held. It was evidently useless out of her presence. Not only had I stopped coming—it was now a year and a half since we had separated—but my ambition to come had left by the basement without saying good-bye. More frequently and intensely than in the years after the accident before Sarah, I was not liking the women who wanted me. There were exceptions—some of those I did not grab at, some of those who did not need me. Some of those I did not grab at, grab at hoping to come up with love, did not dismay me by suddenly turning all one color before my disappointed eyes—all ignorant or banal or helpless or insane. Those I did not grab at, or whose arms of need I did not feel to be encircling my knees, might be ignorant or banal, but if they weren't helpless or insane, if they could see straight, I could, in one case or another, allow them their lovely qualities, even their lovingness, allow them their human spectrum. I could request and value what was difficult about them. Their most important feature, for me, was that they allowed me to allow them to be human.

Most of the women who wanted me struck me as reprisals for damage I'd done their sisters. In one way or another, they were desperate. A number of them grossly parodied fading aspects of me that could never have been so obvious, so conscious-seeming, I *knew*, as I saw them to be in these actresses, their sincerity aflame. I was better than that. I found myself embracing one, two, three, four, five drama-lovers, trouble-makers. They made entrances and exits. They crossed stage left, stopped, turned. They spoke lines. They were witty masochists when not outright tragediennes. Sex was home-theater. They loved excitement, suspense—beginning again, I suppose. I did not believe their emotions. They rehearsed feeling. They wrapped their arms around me. They were alien kin. Their style disgusted me. I undid their arms from me. I undid my arms from them.

The harder I slammed myself against love, having worked up a perfumed steam of ardor, the less I could count on my penis to confirm my zeal. Vaginal doors opened to me. Sorry, wrong house. I did not seem to own my penis. I could not tell it what to do, command it, anymore than I could have raped someone, or physically thrown from my apartment someone who would not leave. But if I had been fucking well, even, as before Sarah, without coming; if my penis had been a prick or cock, reliably stiffenable (did the women who wanted me want me precisely for what I wasn't?), I wouldn't have enjoyed the women I was failing with for more than a day or a week longer than I enjoyed them with my penis half-hearted, easily wet-blanketed. They were the wrong women, not merely not Sarah (most of the time I did not long for Sarah), but not my species, not *mine*, or too much mine. I picked them because they picked me, or I picked them without looking, or with one cell of my brain. There they were. Ignore them? I had to use my freedom, my thirty-eight room house. I might find someone I wanted to need. I had to remain tryable myself. I needed to know that whatever I discovered a woman to be, whatever a woman found out about me, women wanted to try me. I could not stop beginning again. If women did not want me, I was dead. Failing forever I would not be dead. Then I would think: why am I kissing this woman? Because she has lips? I am thirty-eight years old. Or, our clothes off, in bed, the scene laid: what am I doing here with her? She is harmless. I can only do us harm if I don't know or much care who she is. But it's too late now. So, then, for face-saving, a fuck that droops in the sun. I scramble down for a tonguing; I add my thumb. Semen spurts through my fingernail. She comes. I pull myself up for my apology: it takes me a while sometimes, takes me a few times, nothing personal. Next time. Don't worry. She: oh, it takes everybody. . . . It's common. Don't worry.

Because I want her to go, I say, "Why don't you sleep over?" I would sit, the next morning, at my desk reading my newspaper. In my bed, where I had barely slept for the stranger's presence (Sarah and I could sleep embraced, in sunlight, after much coffee), the female turns over and says a lover's sleepy "Hi." She does not belong here. But I have invited her. She has done nothing wrong. But she is cozy. I have "kissed her off" successfully, fluent cunnilinguist. My second book is coming out. I am intelligent, published, a writer. I am so good to talk to. I am understanding, brave, my face sympathetic, trustworthy. I am passionate about serious music. I am "different." I am, perhaps, a find, a catch. All my penis needs is a little time. She will wait for it. The female, naked, comes and sits in the chair by my desk. I give her coffee. She talks. I try to read. She talks. I must be nice. I give up the paper with a small listening smile. She talks on. My ear bleeds. I am so available. She is making love-perpetuating conversation, getting to know me. I say almost nothing. I want to say, "Leave. I need to work this morning." But instead, I freeze her out. It takes another hour, at least. I am so courteously, guiltily cold. I smell of stranger's glue. I want to wash her entirely off me, get to the next glue. The female dresses, at last ("Well, guess I'll be off, I was supposed to meet my girlfriend at eleven"), in a gloomy corner, jerking over her hips the white underpants I had wanted to be so eager to pull down the night before. I am stone. We kiss. "Speak to you soon," I say. She leaves, not yet fully bewildered. It may be that, because I am a writer, I am temperamental, moody. It is worth it, a challenge. I don't speak with her until she telephones, when I excuse myself: work, another woman, "preoccupation." I am relieved. There are men, walking around, with cocks she can swing from. I would think, then: I am, I can be, a lover, loyal, tender. I know it doesn't have to be this way. But where was somebody to stick to? Somebody other than my work? I wanted to need someone, but I needed no one.

In the long time it takes to turn forty (it takes so long that one passes the age well before one reaches it), I began to stop crashing like a compulsive daredevil into vaginal walls. I began to sit stiller, to watch myself using, to watch myself enjoying the use of, my capacity to choose what to do, what not to do, the literary brain, amazingly, used for personal behavior; to *take* time, to consider—to consider oneself, the other, the situation, the combination's prospects, to risk allowing myself to be considered at leisure. Some of my tenderness returned. Remaining independent of psychiatric guidance, I began to learn to let time advise me. I learned that sometimes to let time pass is to use it well; I learned this from writing and I learned it from the cost of rushing. I select my dramas, try, even, to wait, sometimes, for a beloved to arrive. I must hope to revert to recovery. If I don't, I have given up to an invisible dictatorship. I must test for love. I learn, at the same time, that mistakes, if I make fewer, and admit them earlier rather than later, are more forgivable, by me and by the mistaken. I see, too, that I do not make mistakes with others by myself, I do not sing duets alone. I see that I am not the world's mistake-maker. I remember that I am not the world's problem. My penis failing to stay awake in the mouth of a woman I liked but did not trust, I have fallen asleep, the woman, uncharmed, waking me. But I am only another oddity. Some people never come.

I learn to be a less polite mistake-maker. Whatever it is I may give to her, or to him, I am allowed to stop giving it. I am allowed to say I want to stop giving it. *That* is freedom—open refusal. I may say: I regret it, but you are wrong for me. I have made, I am making, a mistake. It is not your fault, it is not mine. I learn to reject the vanity that has made me frightened of my power. I learn that my rejections do not cause plague. I am not Oedipus, a murderer, a bomb.

In the vicinity of forty, I approached my life's permanent conditions. I could see (as far as I could tell from my distance, and not yet knowing the permanent conditions, or whom I would meet among them) that I would write more books, that work might become love. I could see that I was not likely to marry. I would probably decide to be my own wife and my own child, to be enough to care for day to day. My friends, my brother, my sister, had moved into larger apartments, houses, with their children, impressing me. But I would be the bachelor at their dinner tables—a role not beyond the envy of the married. I saw their benefits, as they named their children, as their children began naming their own lives, devising their own flags from their parents' cloth. To be able to share, on the spot, climactic moments—revelations, enthusiasms—was a luxury I would miss and know I was missing. I would miss the two heads that are better than one. I would miss the power of membership in a family of mine, the husband's, the father's, power to entertain, to hearten; but I had my classroom. I would miss being delighted, heartened, by a wife, a child. I would have to tell other families' anecdotes. But I had my friends. I had myself. Living alone, I would have no one to be anxious over me, no one to be anxious over, no one to judge me, no one to judge, no one to make impatient, or patient. I would not, as easily or as often as the married, speak before I could think, saying things too fast and loudly to take back, things that would "have to be forgotten" and might never be forgotten. I would not be insulted by morning noise, or enraged by the bicycle in the driveway. I would not be crowded. I would have privacy and leisure for the making and unmaking of mistakes. I could not be unfaithful, my wife could not be unfaithful, in deed, word, or thought. My wife could not get cancer. There would be no child to inherit my broken neck.

Instead, on a good day in the city of my permanent conditions, where I now live: I have retyped two thousand words of previous days' work. I believe I have hammered out of my new pages all contradictions, redundancies, abstractions, lumpy connections, stubborn softness. The typing may be messy with written interpolations and excisions, but, in the necessary way, the pages are as clean and deserved as diplomas. Flora Tyler, the cleaning woman, has been in to bathe my apartment. Herman Eskin has washed the windows and waxed the floor. It is seven o'clock, a dimming summer evening. An astonishing stream of orange sunset-light appears across my polished floor. It splashes on books, a wooden pepper-mill, into a dull corner, wets my sleeve. A promising dusk. I am praised. I am sitting within a masterpiece. In a few moments, any minute, the doorbell will ring. Three nights before, at a party, I have met someone new—shy, accomplished, just nosy enough, intense but funny, healthy but not wholesome, her own woman. If I made her anxious, she did not show it. I was able to be entertaining. I did not feel I had to belabor my points. She is coming, now, to my house. I am not nervous because I over-love her. I will like what's difficult about her. I will make her look at the orange light. We will go downtown for dinner. I have a reservation. I will perform getting into a taxi. She will be impressed, perhaps relieved, at how easily I do it, but she will say nothing. We will drink, and eat, and then—we do not know. I am, again, beginning again. I am young. I am new. Maybe we will last for the rest of our lives, renew and renew, never wear each other out. Maybe we will have a child, Laurence, after Olivier, Sophie, from *Der Rosenkavalier*. I will bring roses to her and my wife in the hospital. Sarah, after all, taught me how to love. She taught me that I am able to value myself as highly as love requires, as highly as love enables. She taught me my generosity.

Though I could not always use what I learned from her to our benefit, what I learned is there to use. I am not likely ever to distrust the trustworthy as I could distrust Sarah's trustworthiness. I am not likely to submit myself again to the torture of interrogating love as if hoping to force from it the confession that it is not love. If the right beloved—right and independent— were to appear, I could love her, depend now in independence, welcome her entirely.

Someday, some night, any time, love, age, death, will paralyze beginning again. Beginning again is a strategy of my independence. From the time of the accident, first beginning again, I have felt independence as survival. I repeat beginning again because it means escape—from accident, time, repetition, imagined kinds of death and actual death. Though I wanted permanence from Sarah, wanted her to lift me above time, death, accident, I feared obliteration in marriage to her. I felt obliterated, finally, as well as frequently, by *her* marriage; but so long as she was married to someone else, I could not lose all my independence. My mother, my *ad hoc* psychiatrist, tells me how exceptionally winning I was as a child; a woman once warned her not to let me stand at the gate, my winningness would tempt a kidnapper. Thus, a subsequent desire to keep on pleasing. If I keep on pleasing, winning, as I wish I could, I must fear extinction by those I delight; I must fear wanting to be theirs, no longer mine, me. *Bringing Down the House,* I remind myself, is filled with satiric jokes, hostile appeasement. To delight is safety in one direction, hostility is safety in another. My friend Hugh asks my why I worry so about death when I am healthy, only forty, when nothing is wrong. I answer that my fear of death is my fear of being dead while I live. Looking ahead is a way of overlooking whatever in me that is looking for extinction, whatever in me that is already dead or can at any minute die.

Occasionally—less and less, for now—walking into or out of my bathroom, getting into or out of my bed, I fall to the floor. On the ground alone, I am helpless to rise. In my independence, I am always exposed to captivity. In this sense, I live without the net of the former life beneath me. To be alone on the ground suggests how it could have been, dying alone on the road, life out of reach; or lifelong paralysis, fifty years of infancy, the world out of reach. To be alone on the ground suggests how it will be to be dying, to be dead. If the telephone isn't in reach, I slide myself to it. I dial the police emergency number. I sit and wait, or lie and wait, as calmly as if I were reading. (I have never hurt myself falling. My body remembers from its athletic days how to fall.) It is helpful as well as frightening to know I have no choice. Sooner or later, the cops come, carrying walkie-talkies, entering my apartment with a pass-key the doorman has given them. If I am naked, I try to have a towel or shirt over my lap, but the covering is for the cops' sake, not mine, I am beyond embarrassment at these moments, and, in any case, it falls off when I am lifted. I submit to help. I feel as if I am holding my breath against the smell of help until it's done. The cops are calm, too. They return me to my wheelchair. They ask me whether I want to be taken to a hospital. No, everything's fine, I say. Thanks very much for your help. They say, Glad to help, don't mention it. They leave, their walkie-talkies squawking dimly, directing them to fresh emergencies.

Around the time *Bringing Down the House* came out, I dreamed, asleep and awake, that I was being shot at. Shot at through my closed door at home, in my bed or at my desk. Shot at close range at a party. If my book didn't hurt readers, I theorized at the time, if people loved the book, then the book hadn't done its job. But no one shot me. Some people thought the book wonderfully comic, and I was grateful. Some people found it effectively bitter, and I was grateful. It got much more favorable, and much more important, reviews than *The Broken Year* had received, but it did not attract a great many more buyers. It was not debated. In radio interviews, I broadcast its hostility, but it was as if no one wanted to play. The book's prospective audience was in large part the audience the book described, but at the theater I was not recognized, applauded, booed, accosted, berated. I failed to will angry attention, a significant version of the fuss over my Varsity Show review at Middlebury. No one called me "world-beater." No critic called me so much as "Swiftian." I was called, rather, "zany." The shots I dreamed and imagined were real. They scared me. If someone had actually shot me, I would not have been relieved. I wanted noise, not blood, not my blood. I didn't get much more noise than I got blood. Yet, considering the resistance of publishers to the book (they were my audience for two years and a half), its very publication amounted nearly to success.

The bullets coming at me were not fired by anyone I recognized, or by any*one*. The bullets, I figured out, had been fired from the ambush all writers must pass at publication, that ambush, in the case of *The Broken Year,* having been the missiles in Cuba. I was, for days, about to be assassinated by fate, or time, or rivalry—perhaps, to stop me from "acting up," by my dead father—just as I was about to make it to the safety of fame, success, legend. When I zoomed in taxis through the transverses of Central Park, the headlights of taxis coming around turns from the other direction seemed to be aiming at me. Everything was bullets.

I did not fail to make it to the safety of legend because I got shot. My imagination was inaccurate, the assassins were inaccurate. But I had learned, and would soon be learning more, about emergency, how fresh it kept. While I was a writer, and, like anyone risking success, could fear getting knocked off the wire as success becomes reachable, or half-hope to get knocked off the wire, I had collected other reasons, after my accident, for anticipating danger. Even knowing that danger, like time, keeps its plans secret, comes from directions too oblique or too direct, too predictable, to chart, comes faster than one can get out of the way, or comes aimed not at you at all but at others, I continue to anticipate danger. And for all my preventive fear, dangers come true.

Ever since the accident, I have been absorbed—impressed, entertained, stricken—by fate's outwitting of hope or hopelessness, by the brutality of coincidence or the pointedly inappropriate. My early love for the performance of slapstick, my own and my friends' on the street, the enviable Marx Brothers' in the movies, revived as speculation after the accident, after slapstick began cutting up within my life. When I'd been in the hospital in Burlington a few weeks, a large tile in the ceiling dislodged and fell, missing my head by a foot. One of the first letters I received after the accident was from my earliest childhood playmate, who had starred with me in a recurrent early nightmare of mine—it was this nightmare that first told me I would die one day—in which two Japanese soldiers, coming through a distant gate in my grandparents' meadow, advanced on us, seeking us out with bayoneted rifles as we shivered behind a rock. I hadn't seen my friend in years. What a terrible thing has happened to you, he wrote, pressing an icy hand to my heart. (How did he know it was terrible? It had happened to me. I didn't think it was terrible.) Subsequently, following an automobile accident, he died. I wrote to his parents. In the early sixties, I myself was in another automobile accident, harmless to bodies, as it turned out, but suggestively damaging to the cars involved.

I visit the mother of an old friend for dinner. We talk about cancer, our dread of it. She says she would kill herself if she found she had it. The next year, she has cancer. She does not bother to kill herself. I visit her shortly before she dies. I watch the worst coming true for others. Two more friends, contemporaries, die of cancer. A most beloved friend, standing on a sidewalk, is hit by a taxi. In the waiting room of the hospital a group of friends is waiting with her husband while doctors try to save her. My friend Hugh comes in. We stare at each other for ten locked seconds, in horror. Reports are delivered, graver and graver. At one of them, the one before her death, we in the waiting room peel away from one another and weep. Tragedy off the stage, in the audience. I have never received such pain. I know now what it was like in the waiting room at my hospital. But I did not die. It is as if I did not begin to believe in death until it happened to enough others to be a possibility. I will not yet be convinced of death. I am a death agnostic. I do not cross out of my personal phone book numbers and addresses of friends who have died. Buying a new phone book, I transfer their numbers and addresses to it. When I leave a funeral, I leave it for somewhere else, as if I had been visiting someone ill, as if death were an illness the dead will get over. I think about death to convince myself of death and to remind myself that I am alive. At those moments when I am convinced of death, I do not try, I do not wish to try, to put it, or me, "in perspective." It consoles me not at all, as my scientist father told me it consoled him, to know that cellular multiplication continues after we, individually, die, that "life goes on." I am not one of those who realize, looking up at the stars, how insignificant I am in the total scheme of things. I like looking, or glancing, up at the stars well enough, but I am not interested in how many there are, and how far away they are. They are very far away, and there are very many of them. I'm here, and there's only one of me. When I go, I'm gone, missing out forever, missing the promise of the orange light.

I attended a performance of *Der Rosenkavalier*. Sophie and Octavian were singing their final duet. When they finished, they would run offstage to a long life together, a happy ending. They jerked my tears. I was in love with them. Two elderly women, several rows ahead of mine, stood in the middle of the duet. They swayed, in a painstaking sashay, considerate of knees, toward their aisle. The lovers were blacked out, I was blinded. I walloped the back of the seat in front of me with my fist, plenty of strength for that. The man in the seat turned in alarm to see what was happening to him. The two old women trekked up the aisle, toward me in my aisle seat. I said to them, in a shouted whisper, "What are you *doing?*" They ignored me, passed on. The next night, I dreamed I was crouching in a tall hut made of two-by-fours. Through the large cracks, I could see one Japanese soldier scrambling over the wood, holding his bayoneted rifle, looking for me. They had already found my playmate. I had not had the dream since my childhood.

No amount of wariness, or experience, helps. Nothing, no one, can stop a plane from crashing into the Empire State Building, or a barbell from falling off a windowsill onto the head, far below, of a man who has just left a first-class restaurant after an anniversary lunch with his wife and is saying to her, "That was expensive, all right, but it sure was worth it." Nothing more is supposed to happen to me, I still sometimes suppose, unwilling to release the expectation of immortality with which I began my second life. But things happen, things will happen. Bullets fire. Barbells fall. Cars collide. Planes hit buildings. Cars climb sidewalks. Cancer arrives. Someday I may fall and be unable to call for help, or help will be unable to hear me. If I were time, accident, danger, death, I could prevent them.

I am the classic "self-made man." I am proud of my distance from the days of my physical poverty. I cherish those who have struggled. Independence is survival, survival is success. I escaped "the" accident, death, the state of illness, fifty years of infancy, being "taken care of." But what I escaped, I must keep behind me. I will not outgrow my fear of anxious or proprietary people. There are women in wheelchairs at the opera who look to me like potatoes. In full health, I imagine minor ailments to be dangerous symptoms, or else, from fear, ignore them away. I do not submit routinely to preventive medicine. What may it not show up?

So, in my wheelchair I am grand but anxious. I am often—and often resist being—controlling. I try to avoid getting angry, or stimulating others to anger. Having once upset the applecart, it is best, or seems best, not to rock the boat. In personal and political matters, I try, privately, to visit the other side. It is a way of taking nothing for granted, of being watchful, of watching myself. I watch myself. I watch what I am doing.

But I forget, most of the time, to be anxious, or grand. I take sides, get angry, make enemies, commit. I am energetic. And the boat doesn't sink. I have, for the most part, come to trust the value of what I give and what I accept, and to accept what I have cost. A month after the accident, I dreamed I was sitting in a wheelchair in an attic. My father was sitting beside me. I asked him if I was hurt. He said, "You are completely ruined." On an April evening six years later, my father visited me in my apartment. He lay on my bed; I sat beside him in my wheelchair. We chatted and joked, at our best together. Two days later, he died. Twelve years after he died, I dreamed that my father was saying to me, "I am holding you in all my arms."